Good Morning
Aztlán

GOOD MORNING

Aztlán

THE WORDS, PICTURES & SONGS OF
LOUIE PÉREZ

TIA CHUCHA PRESS

Book Design: Jane Brunette
Original Book Design: Rodolfo Arana
Cover art and inside art: Louie Pérez

PUBLISHED BY:
Tia Chucha Press
A Project of Tía Chucha's Centro Cultural, Inc. PO Box 328
San Fernando, CA 91341
www.tiachucha.org

DISTRIBUTED BY:
Northwestern University Press
Chicago Distribution Center
11030 South Langley Avenue
Chicago IL 60628

Tia Chucha's Centro Cultural & Bookstore is a 501 (c) (3) nonprofit corporation funded in part over the years by the National Endowment for the Arts, California Arts Council, Los Angeles County Arts Commission, Los Angeles Department of Cultural Affairs, The California Community Foundation, the Annenberg Foundation, the Weingart Foundation, the Lia Fund, National Association of Latino Arts and Culture, Ford Foundation, MetLife, Southwest Airlines, the Andy Warhol Foundation for the Visual Arts, the Thrill Hill Foundation, the Middleton Foundation, Center for Cultural Innovation, John Irvine Foundation, Not Just Us Foundation, the Attias Family Foundation, and the Guacamole Fund, Arts for Justice Fund, among others. Donations have also come from Bruce Springsteen, John Densmore of The Doors, Jackson Browne, Lou Adler, Richard Foos, Gary Stewart, Charles Wright, Adrienne Rich, Tom Hayden, Dave Marsh, Jack Kornfield, Jesus Trevino, David Sandoval, Gary Soto, Denise Chávez and John Randall of the Border Book Festival, Luis & Trini Rodríguez, and more.

For my mother and father:
Guadalupe Zepeda Pérez and Louis Frausto Pérez Sr.

You are in my heart and in everything I do.

LOS LOBOS 1982

TABLE OF CONTENTS

PREFACE

It seems like it was just a day ago that I was riding my Schwinn Sting Ray bike around the streets of my busy neighborhood in East Los Angeles, singing along with the songs playing on the red plastic transistor radio that was taped to the handle bars.

Looking back, there were two radios playing in the background of my young life.

There was the brown Bakelite Zenith on the counter by the blender in my mother's kitchen that she had tuned permanently to one Spanish-language AM station. It woke us up early every morning to the sound of rancheras as many other radios did throughout Mexican Los Angeles. That radio serenaded my mom as she toasted French bread on the iron comál and made coffee in an old dented tin percolator.

Then there was the other radio—the one that was attached to my blue bicycle, about the size of the pack of Camels my uncle Manuel smoked as he lay on the old green army cot in the tiny back room at my abuelita's house. That radio cranked out the sounds of The Miracles, The Four Tops, The Rolling Stones, and Jimi Hendrix as well as other not-so-old-at-the time-oldies.

Music was all around me in my neighborhood. There was everything from car stereos blasting rhythm and blues out of midnight blue low-riding Chevy Impalas to the sweet angelic sounds of the choir rehearsing in the church hall across the street. It soon became clear to me music is something special.

In the beginning I never imagined music would become a big part of who I am. What started as a spark turned into a full-blown fire. It changed my perspective, the way I looked at what surrounded me. The gritty reality I saw in my East L.A. barrio became poetic and beautiful.

In the dreams that sometimes dissolved into bitterness and regret, there was poetry. In the smog-shrouded lavender sunsets along the horizon of downtown Los Angeles, I saw a thing of beauty. I heard the music of joy and promise as I rode my bike past the house where a newborn baby was crying. I saw the look of hope and wonder on the faces of children as they walked to their first day of school.

Not long after high school in 1973, Cesar Rosas, David Hidalgo, Conrad Lozano, and myself formed Los Lobos. That band subsequently took me out of my little neighborhood to every corner of the United States and to countries all around the world.

For all these many years I've been writing songs, making music, and, when I can find the time from my crazy schedule, draw squiggly lines on paper and make paintings.

As I reflect on it now, it's been quite a journey on that blue bike. And what I have to show for it is a good sized collection of writings, poems, and pictures that serve as a reminder of where I've been, what I've seen, and the dreams I think we've all had. Now I've gathered a selection of songs and art, put them in some kind of order, the way a young boy on the brink of adolescence might gather up his toys and other evidence of his youth, and make some sense of what all those "things" mean. I'm very happy to share them with you in this little book that has become a lyrical memoir of life.

I hope that you all enjoy the ride as much as I did.

ACKNOWLEDGMENTS: It is no easy task to take the bits and pieces of one's artistic life and assemble them in some order when the subject is in constant motion. So the process of putting together this book wasn't easy. As a working musician, I'm moving at a high rate of speed for most of my waking hours, only to lay my head down to sleep for a short while in a hotel bed somewhere between point A and point Z. I'd like to thank all of those who stayed with me on this project and helped to finally get this thing between two covers.

First I'd like to thank my editor and dear friend Luis Torres for his patience and insightful understanding of the material that went into this book. His skill as a writer and editor was invaluable. Thanks to Rodolfo Arana who came up with this idea because he believed that it was time to put it down for posterity. His work as a visual artist and his dedication to the creative calling continues to inspire me. Thanks to my musical brother and songwriter-without-equal Dave Alvin for taking the time to write some kind words. You rock like no other. Thank you David Greenberger for another great conversation about life, music, and the joy of making squiggly lines on a piece of paper. I'm glad that toll calls are a thing of the past. Gracias to my *hermano* Luis J. Rodríguez— amazing writer, poet, and founder of Tía Chucha Press—for his incredible patience and commitment to this book and, above all, for his tireless work for the Chicano community. And to Martha González for years of friendship, and whose energy and talent is a constant inspiration.

My special thanks to David Hidalgo, my friend and songwriting accomplice of almost fifty years—and to the rest of the members of my musical family, Los Lobos: Conrad, Cesar, and Steve Berlin. Where would I be without you all? Probably home more often.

And last, and certainly most importantly, I want to thank my loving wife Mary who allowed me to be away from home for most of our married life, who believed in me and put up with all my crazy dreams. Thanks for leaving the light on for me, *mi amor.* I want to express my gratitude to my boys: Louis, John, and Matthew. They never learned from my mistakes but instead had the courage to make some of their own. They are brilliant and incredible. In addition, I want to acknowledge my sister Carmen for sharing a life with me. Maybe we'll grow up one day, but we're in no hurry. Finally, I can't forget all of my friends and fans. I'm endlessly grateful for your love and support. I couldn't have done any of this without you.

Thanks.

—*Louie Pérez*

INTRODUCTION

■ *by Luis Torres*

LOUIE PÉREZ AND I hit it off right away when we met a lifetime ago.

It all began with a phone call some forty years ago. I was just out of college and I was working on a little documentary film with a good friend who had a bit more experience with filmmaking than I did. His name was Rudy Vargas. He'd just gotten out of UCLA film school. It was the first film I'd ever worked on. We needed someone to play some music for the film. Vargas gave me a phone number. He said, "There are some young guys who play beautiful Mexican music. They look like hippies, but they play like El Trio Los Panchos." He asked me to call them up and see if we could get them to record some music for the little movie.

The phone number he gave me was Louie Pérez's home number. (There were no cell phones then.) There was no Internet yet, but that's a different story.

I dialed the number and Louie answered. That's how we met. We've had thousands of telephone conversations since then. Those hippie-looking young Chicano musicians eventually became Los Lobos. Louie was—and still is—a vital part of that remarkable band's creativity.

Those phone conversations continue today. Whether he calls from down the street or from Paris or Tokyo, we always pick up where we left off. We are friends. We share each other's stories, secrets, and lies. And we always find something to laugh about. I've gotten to know Louie well. We trust each other and that's why it was such a pleasure to collaborate with him on this book project.

When the idea for this book first came up, he picked up the phone and gave me a call. That's how I came to be involved in this endeavor. I've been a journalist and editor all of my adult life and I was pleased to lend Louie a hand.

Over the past couple of years I've been pleased to help Louie cobble this book together, sorting through the hundreds of songs and poems he's written over the years, working earnestly to develop some order out of the clutter of lyric sheets and notebooks nestled in cardboard boxes in garages and closets. And now, this book is ready for the reader. It may enlighten. It may surprise. It may perplex. But I believe it is sure to be an eye-opening and enjoyable journey for the reader. In this book, others will speak specifically of his prodigious gifts as a writer and of his explorations as a visual artist. I know him as the individual who is at the core of those talents.

Louie Pérez is at once a complex fellow and a simple man.

He's quietly intelligent. Loves to read. He's amused by the ironies and foibles of people and societies that confront us every day. He is driven by curiosity and a desire to make sense of—or at least understand—the craziness of the world around us. But above all, he is driven by a desire, no a need, to explore— to use his imagination to create words and music and pictures. There is an unbridled passion for art that propels him to do what he does. And he does it well, as this little book will attest. And in all the years I've known him, he has always been stricken with a genuine sense of wonder. We question everything all around us while we simultaneously embrace the beauty and joy that can be found in this world, even in the most unlikely places.

Louie Pérez has the ability to see beauty that is hidden from many folks. He can scan the cracked and broken pavement on a street in East Los Angeles with a knowing eye. Others will only see disfigurement, ugliness. But he has the capacity to see the beauty in the patterns and designs that the mangled concrete can evoke. And he has the vision to capture that kind of hidden beauty in his words and pictures. It's quite a gift. Perhaps it's also a curse. But that's his perspective. And we, the music lover, the lover of art in all its dimensions, are all the better for it.

Enjoy this ride with Louie as your guide.

Luis Torres *is a veteran journalist and author from L.A.'s eastside.*

one

SOMETHING LIKE JOY

RUDY'S PARTY

THERE WERE ROSES growing in a patch by the screen door, on the pink steps potted spearmint fixed our stomachs when too much cake and Jell-O kept us up at night. Little Rudy's party went on and on and on, even after Rudy fell asleep, tired from running circles in the brown grass, too exited about anything, not knowing or caring about turning five.

I guess everything looks so big when you're that small. Huge shoes coming through the house singing *"déjame morir."* Uncle Pancho whistled and tio Benny wore that dumb-looking straw hat and always put on cowboy boots when he got drunk, stunk bad in our faces saying *"Ay que chulo."*

Oh yeah, and Manuel could fly. Well, he said he could, only when the moon was full or more like when his belly was full of cough medicine and beer. The hot dogs and bread tasted good, but the beans had fat chunks of onion that made me sneeze. My grandma likes 'em that way, with a big orange soda on the side, so I made a plate to take to her, because she can't come out no more.

Some of the presents were wrapped in the Sunday funny papers, some wrapped in the white butcher stuff you get at Carbajal's Dandy Market, but Rudy won't be opening them today, he's too little and sleepy, I'll bet he'll be up real early tomorrow, before the pots line up at the corner for soup and eyes are too red to get out of bed. Everybody got silly and somebody got very stupid that long day, but the sky forgave and the clouds moved away, making it all right.

"Happy Birthday to you," the rooster cried.

"Happy Birthday for you," the birds sang up in the palm trees.

"And have a nice life," all the neighbors shouted.

And for miles around, car horns honked and lunch wagons tooted their goofy songs, even the church bell rang five times for Rudy, and one more time for good luck.

Rudy had a shirt
with the whole world
on it.
there was mountains
and deserts and countries

ALL THE
EVERY
WHERE

PLACES
WAS ON
his
shiRT.

SAINT BEHIND THE GLASS

◼ THE SIGHTS AND SMELLS OF MY CHILDHOOD
HOME ON HAMMEL STREET IN EAST L.A.

Hammer and a nail
Hammer and a nail
Saint behind the glass
Holds a hammer and a nail

Baby in his arms
Baby in his arms
Saint behind the glass
Has a baby in his arms

Watches me sleep
Watches me sleep
Saint behind the glass
Watches me while I sleep

Coffee in the air
Coffee in the air
Saint behind the glass
Smells coffee in the air

Curtains blowing 'round
Curtains blowing 'round
Saint behind the glass
Sees the curtains blowing 'round

Night upon my head
Night upon my head
Saint behind the glass
Lays night upon my head

Mother don't cry
Mother don't cry
Saint behind the glass
Tells mother not to cry

LIFE IS GOOD

■ LIFE IS SOMETIMES NOT SO GOOD, HUH?
BUT THAT'S OKAY.

I get happy 'cause my life is good
I get laughing 'cause I know I should
I get all happy 'cause my life is good, so good

I get happy 'cause my life is good
Turning out just like I thought it would
I get all happy 'cause my life is so damn good
And I go
Ooh la la Mmm Ooh la la…

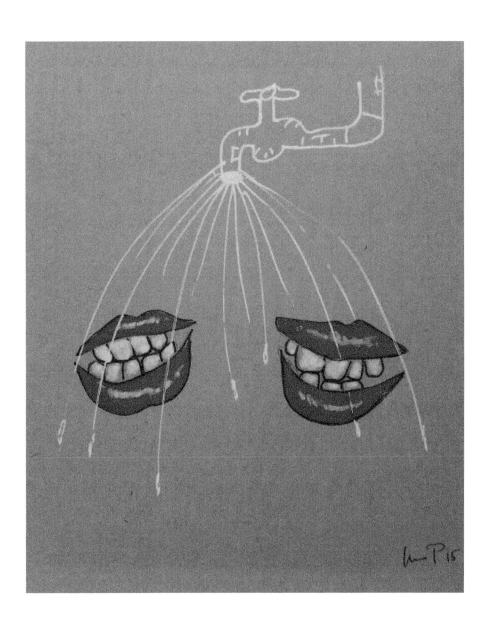

LA PLAYA

■ WE GO TO THE BEACH TO STAND AT THE EDGE
OF THE EARTH AND WONDER HOW WE GOT HERE.

Vamos a la playa
Con Rosita, Sandra y Juan
Vamos a la playa
Con Rosita, Sandra y Juan
Aunque el agua sea fría
Vamos a tener mucho fun
Aunque el agua sea fría
Vamos a tener mucho fun

Vamos a la playa
Vamos a la playa

Vamos a nadar hasta
La isla de la mujer
Vamos a nadar hasta
La isla de la mujer
Allí podemos correr desnudos
Porque nadie nos puede ver
Allí podemos correr desnudos
Porque nadie nos puede ver

Vamos a la playa
Vamos a la playa

TILL THE HANDS FALL OFF THE CLOCK

■ WHEN YOU'RE WITH SOMEONE YOU CARE ABOUT, MAYBE A LOVER OR A GOOD FRIEND, THAT'S WHEN THE CLOCK STOPS TICKING.

And love is waiting for you and I
Let's stay up and forget about getting up
Tonight is just about you and me
There's nowhere else to go
And no one will ever know
And we'll dance this way
Till the hands fall off the clock

Listen to your heart
'Cause hearts never lie
Leave your cares behind
For someone else to find

LEMON 'N ICE

■ WOULDN'T IT BE NICE IF WE JUST LISTEN TO EACH OTHER?

Wouldn't it be nice
To have a lemon 'n ice
And you never have to say you care for me

Wouldn't it be right
If we could have all night
And say that you'll never miss me

Couldn't I just say
If you think it's okay
That you never have to need me

I won't have to know
If late at night you go
And you can pretend that you never knew me

Like a lemon 'n ice
Wouldn't it be nice
To take the cool with the heat
And the sour and the sweet

LUNA

■ ONE NIGHT, WHEN I WAS A LITTLE KID, I WENT OUT INTO THE
BACKYARD AND LOOKED UP AT A FULL MOON THAT SEEMED TO
FILL THE ENTIRE SKY. WE HAD A CONVERSATION.

Luna baila
Baila en el cielo
Tengo que bailar con ti

Luna canta
Canta en el cielo
Tengo que cantar con ti

Luna lejos
Luna de consuelo
Ven cantar aquí con mi

Luna bella
Luna de mi alma
Ven acércate a mi

THE GIVING TREE

■ Ribbons, warm wind, and baby hands—very happy stuff.

A warm wind is blowing through the valleys and the mountain tops
Down the road to a place we know so well
The children are running with ribbons in their baby hands
While we all gather 'round the Giving Tree

Let's go sing songs, the blue ones
Let's go sing about the Lord above
And thank the old sun for all we have
The sad times, the glad times
The babies swinging in our arms
Just don't seem much like rain 'round the Giving Tree

Like the shepherds once followed a star bright up in the sky
We're all here to say: come be with us now
Come give us a good one
Come give us a happy time
While we're all here to dance 'round the Giving Tree

ANGEL DANCE

■ I REMEMBER A PLAID BLANKET AND A PILLOW IN A
ONE-BEDROOM HOUSE IN EAST L.A. THIS IS A LULLABY
FOR SOMEONE WHO IS AFRAID OF THE DARK.

And they'll laugh up and down the hall
Don't you go shout when you hear them fall
Let them fly across the wall
Let them cry until the morning calls
Little two-step angel dance
Good night, sleep tight
The big bright sun has gone away
Done gone away
Goodbye, don't cry
Tomorrow will bring us a brand new day
We can run and play
Big night, bright lights
Time now to lay them all to rest
Put them all to rest
Bad guys, mean eyes
All gone away to where they belong
Let's just sing our song
Good days, new ways
Let go of all things when you sleep
When you're all asleep
Good night, sleep right
Tomorrow is going to bring us another day
So we can run and play

And they'll laugh up and down the hall
Don't you go shout when you hear them fall
Let them fly across the wall
Let them cry until the morning calls
Little two-step angel dance

WHEN WE WERE FREE

■ ONCE UPON A TIME WE WERE INNOCENT AND FREE—
AND WE STILL CAN BE.

I can still feel that moment
That so-tender moment
When we would run and laugh

We'd sing about it
Even shout about it
Didn't care about what they would say

It was all we wanted
All we needed
And never had to feel afraid

I can almost touch it
Can almost hold it
Now slipped so ever far away

We forgot that moment
That so-precious moment
And let this world steal it from you and me

I remember you laughing
So long ago when we were free

mi hermana y
yo como
niños

In the
Sun
in 1956

THE PURPLE MOON

■ HE FELT REAL SAD AND HE FELT REAL GLAD.

the telephone woke him early in the morning, he sat up and giggled and listened to it ring and ring until it stopped ringing, somebody knocked at the door so he went over, peeked through the window and watched them knock and knock until they stopped knocking and went away, he made his way across the kitchen, around the table to the back door and let the birds out one by one, first the brown one, then the white one and then the one with the funny spots on his head, he watched them soar up into the sky till they were just specks in the blue, he climbed the ladder up the side of the garage to get a better look and saw them float far, far away, he felt real sad and real glad.

too soon the night came and he lifted the shades as the moon came over the fence, it was kind of purple and bright, and it scared him a little bit, so he went out and stood on the grass and stared right up at it to show himself he wasn't afraid, they made friends real quick and the cat came over to see what was going on, the two of them went back into the house and turned out the lights so the moon could come in and laid down and went to sleep.

the telephone woke them early the next morning, they sat up and laughed and listened to it ring and ring till it stopped ringing.

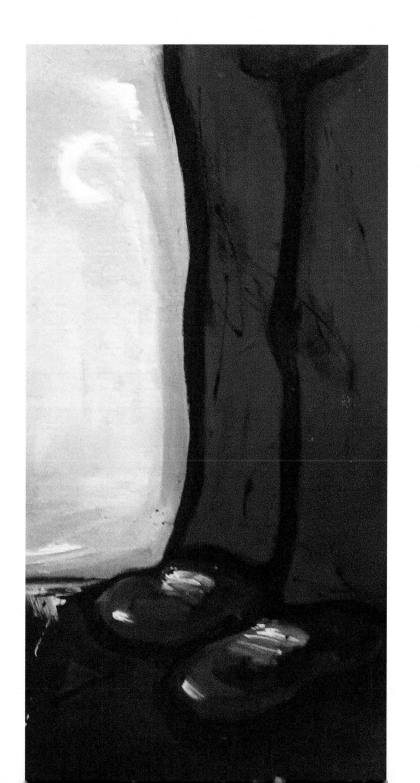

two

LOST SOULS AND HAUNTED HEARTS

MARGIE'S HEART

■ HOW DO YOU GO ON LIVING WHEN A CHUNK
OF YOUR HEART APPEARS TO BE GONE?

There were pieces of a broken heart scattered around the yard in front of Margarita's house. It didn't look like Margie had made it through the screen door last night with all her vital organs intact. It was quite a messy scene.

Something started swelling inside her chest months ago when she first met Raul at Maldonado's Mini Mart by the cemetery on Downey Road. He seemed so right and so terribly wrong when she first eyed him from top to bottom, but it was the sound of his voice that was like a beautiful bolero playing in her ears that convinced her heart to beat to the rhythm of his song. But soon after dances were danced, kisses were kissed, hands were held and promises exchanged, he left. She waited and waited but he never returned. So here we are, John, Lucha, Elena Rios and Paul, on her lawn picking up pieces of her poor broken corazón. After two hours of searching through the weeds, we were lucky to find almost all the parts except for one.

Margarita Consuelo Chávez would have to go on through her life with that one piece missing.

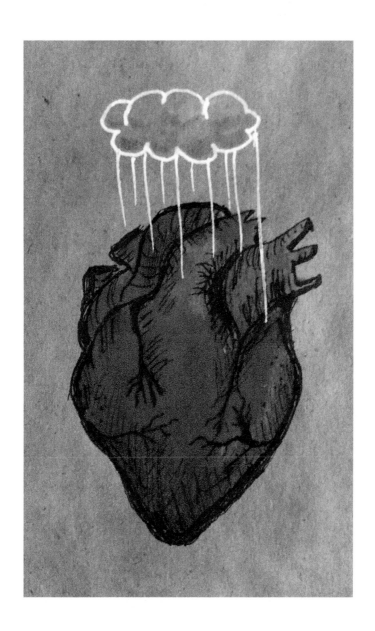

MADE TO BREAK YOUR HEART

■ WHAT SOUND DOES A HEART MAKE WHEN IT IS BREAKING?

What was it that I heard making sounds
Moving around in the night
In the second dream I had you were gone
Disappeared out of sight

I didn't know what to say to you

You think it's like a river flowing
You better know that love is made to break your heart

I was walking down the shore
With a wish held tight in my hand
Then the sea came along
And washed away our names in the sand

I didn't know what to say to you

You think it's like a river flowing
Don't you know that love is made to break your heart

What was it that you said
When your hair fell down in your eyes
You didn't even care to find the words
To tell me goodbye

I didn't know what to say to you

You think it's like a river flowing
Don't you know that love is made to break your heart

REVA'S HOUSE

■ WE ALL WONDERED WHAT WAS GOING ON AT THE HOUSE NEXT DOOR.

Maybe it was the way he walked
Or the way he combed his hair
Could have been the fancy words
Or the sweet wine in the air

Wasn't the muddy shoes she'd hear
Slow coming up the hall
Or the faces in the pictures
That were hanging on the wall

Knock down the door to Reva's house
There's something going on
The dogs were barking late last night
There's something going wrong

Maybe she hoped he would just go away
And she'd wake up alone in bed
Maybe there was no reason
For the things that he had said

Didn't find the matches
Couldn't light them in the dark
Could only hear the sound
Of the breaking of her heart

Don't know where to run to
I don't know where to hide
Can't hold my head up anymore
Don't listen when I cry

Knock down the door to Reva's house
There's something going on
The dogs were barking late last night
There's something going wrong

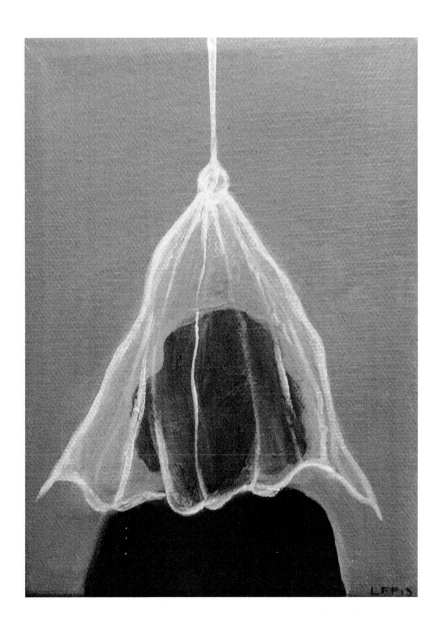

DOWN ON THE RIVERBED

■ Took a walk with his lover.

Down on the riverbed
Down on the riverbed
Down on the riverbed
I asked my lover for her hand

A red-tailed hawk circled overhead
A red-tailed hawk circled overhead
A red-tailed hawk circled overhead
"The church on the hill" is what she said

A monster cloud like a big black hand
A monster cloud like a big black hand
A monster cloud like a big black hand
As she drew houses in the sand

Then I heard a train whistle blow
Then I heard a train whistle blow
Then I heard a train whistle blow
And I knew it was time to go

THE CIRCUS COMES TO TOWN

■ TWO FRIENDS, ONE LOVE, NOW GONE AWAY.

Could have had a chance to get out of this wreck
The time that you came and the day that you left
Could have had a chance
Could have had a chance

Never thought I could make it this far
With a dent in my soul and a hole in my heart
Never thought I could
Never thought I could

But when the lights are turning 'round
And wheels are rolling on the ground
That day I'll burn this whole place down
When the circus comes to town

You left your name carved on a tree
You scratched mine out right in front of me
Didn't mean that much
Didn't mean that much

I'll scratch your name out on that tree
I'll chase your heart right out of me
Doesn't mean that much
Doesn't mean that much

But when the lights are turning 'round
And wheels are rolling on the ground
That day I'll burn this whole place down
When the circus comes to town

TWO JANES

■ ON A PLANE COMING HOME FROM SOMEWHERE, I READ IN THE NEWS-
PAPER A TRAGIC STORY ABOUT TWO YOUNG GIRLS WHO DECIDED TO END
THEIR LIVES. I WROTE THIS SONG.

Two Janes running along the tracks
Saying "We don't want to live this way
Ain't never coming back"

Jane number one looked as happy as can be
Jane number two knew what could set them free
Too many nights hiding under beds
Too many fears to fill their pretty heads
Everybody knows they must have been insane
So goes the tale of two Janes

Tears falling down behind the bedroom door
"No matter how I try, I just don't know what for
Too many times, I'm banging into walls
Too many times, I cry but no one ever calls"
Everybody knows they must have been insane
So goes the tale of two Janes

Jane number one is standing at the gate
Jane number two has the key that holds their fate
Too many angels with brand new silken wings
Too many cries for love but no one hears a thing
Everybody knows they must have been insane
So goes the tale of two Janes

BOY BRUISED BY BUTTERFLY CHASE

■ A YOUNG CHILD PURSUES A BUTTERFLY
AND RUNS OFF OF A CLIFF.

Someone was laughing at me
At me without shoes
But the grass felt so good
And the day was so blue

Must have tripped, I don't know
Do I remember falling away?
Nothing that I hold onto and not being afraid

Down, down, down
Falling down, down, down
It's like I was born never to touch the ground

Someone was crying while I lay in the dirt
I could hear their hearts breaking
But I wasn't even hurt

Down, down, down,
Falling down, down, down

It's like I was born never touching the ground
Ground, ground
Like I was born never touching the ground

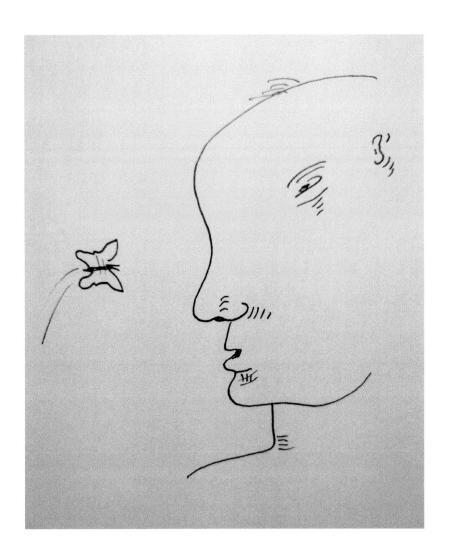

EVANGELINE

■ A GIRL, A DREAM, AND A SIGH.

Evangeline is on her own
Just barely seventeen
When she left home
She don't know where she is
Or where she's going
She is the queen of make believe, Evangeline

I can still remember this little girl
Black eyes just staring
At this big old world
Ran off to find some American dream
Train ticket in one hand
In her new blue jeans

She went out dancing on a Saturday night
Silk stockings and high heels
Blue liner on her eyes
But on Sunday morning she's all alone
Head lying near the nightstand
By the telephone

Evangeline is on her own
Just barely seventeen
When she left home
She don't know where she is
Or where she's going

She is the queen of make believe, Evangeline

DONE GONE BLUE

■ In case you're wondering why they call it the blues.

> Oh sweet mystery
> Strung together along a wire
> But then it breaks—why I don't know
> What is there to do
> When this thing's done gone blue
>
> Oh sweet majesty
> Diamond studded in the mire
> Oh how it shines—until the end of time
> How is it for you
> When this thing's done gone blue
>
> Oh yeah sweet agony
> When the last coal's in the fire
> How long it burns—well I don't know
> What are you gonna do
> When this thing's done gone blue
> This thing's done gone blue

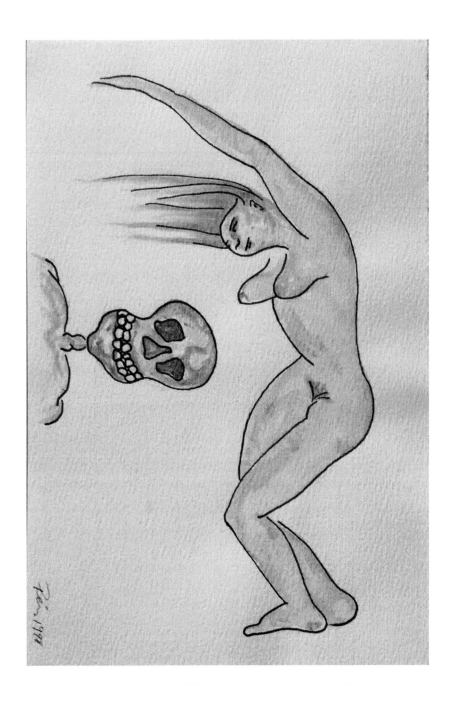

ALICIA LETTER

■ SOMETIMES THE EASIEST LETTERS TO WRITE ARE THE ONES THAT AREN'T SENT. SOMETIMES THE HARDEST LETTERS TO WRITE ARE THE ONES THAT YOU WON'T SEND.

I didn't know what to do
When I saw a hundred miles between
Me and you
That it wasn't good
And it wasn't bad
It wasn't happy
And it wasn't sad
I couldn't find the words to say
"Let's have it now and not yesterday"
That it wasn't me
And it wasn't you
That it wasn't heartache
And it wasn't blue
If I knew then as I do now
I would have paid a million
To find out how
To make it last
To make it stay
Instead of tossing it all away

IF

■ THE OCEAN IN A BOTTLE.

    If we stood by the river or by the sea
    If we stood by the river or there by the sea
    If I couldn't swim would you laugh at me

    If the ocean was wine or full of gin
    If the ocean was whiskey or filled with gin
    Would you lead me away or would you push me in

    Would you push me in

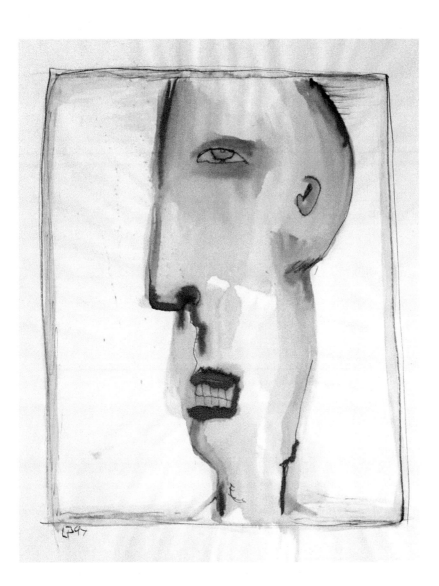

JUST A MAN

■ HE WOULD CHANGE THINGS IF HE COULD.

Just a man made of blood and bone
I've thrown away all that was once my own

Old and worn and tired too
Of cold so cold and blue so blue

Endless love washed away in the sand
Too much to lose for just a man

In my time I never had my fill
Of breaking hearts for just a thrill

Letting love run through my hands
Too much to lose for just a man

Don't put too many
Cards on this hard-headed man
Take whatever is yours
And get as far away as you can

No gray clouds lined with silver and gold
No little boy to watch me grow

I played the game as I know I can
So much to ache so much to break
Too much at stake for just a man

LITTLE THINGS

■ NOW THAT I'M OLDER MAYBE NOW I'M THINKING
ABOUT GETTING INTO HEAVEN.

I've scaled the highest mountain
Crossed the deep blue sea
Chased that mighty, mighty dollar
Dreamed of the man that I could be

Little things all around me
Little things that I could never see
Like the love you tried to give me
And in the end, just threw away

I stood atop the golden tower
Rode upon a silver steed
Piled the riches higher and higher
More then a man could ever need

Little things all around me
Little things that I could never see
Like the heart beating inside me
That I just threw away

Those little things all around me
Little things I never learned to see
Like the love you tried to give me
I went ahead and threw it away

Little things all around me
Little things that I could never see
Like the heart breaking inside me
I just threw it away

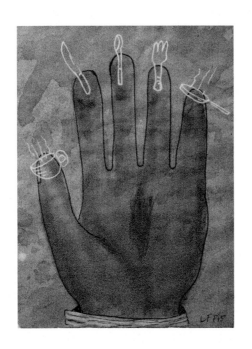

RITA

■ I WISH THEY HAD TAUGHT US MORE ABOUT
DISAPPOINTMENT WHEN WE WERE YOUNG.

The radio's on, the song they play
Can't make no sense of what they say
I couldn't tell you if I knew

Don't understand most things I see
In the blue light of the TV
I couldn't tell you what to do

Rita, it all just seems too much
And sometimes maybe not enough
My head is so, so filled up

And Rita, I guess I think too much
Or maybe sometimes not enough
My head is always so filled up

I hold the phone close to my ear
Can't recognize the voice I hear
Couldn't remember what they said

The newspaper stacks up on the step
I can't believe how long I slept
Now why should I get out of bed?

Rita, it all just seems too much
And sometimes maybe not enough
My head is so, so filled up

And Rita, I guess I think too much
Or maybe sometimes not enough
My head is always so filled up

There was a thing floating way up there
Was it a wish or another prayer
It was just stuck, stuck up in the air

DON'T DISAPPEAR

■ HOMEBOYS AND PHYSICS AND TECHNOLOGY AND MEDICINE
AND FAITH AND LOVE.

"I think I'm disappearing, Homes," says Little Rooster to Raydog. They're sitting on blue plastic milk crates in front of Bill's Shop & Save, across from the church on Hammel Street. "Sometimes I feel like I'm not in my body, like I'm looking at myself from somewheres else."

"What are you talking about, Roost?" Ray is staring at him over the top of his shades.

"I swear to god, bro. It happens all of a sudden and this morning when I was eating my Lucky Charms, it was like I wasn't there."

"That's just too weird, Rooster."

Louie Avila and Ray Cortez have known each other since the fourth grade. Louie got the nickname "Rooster" when he showed up late for school one morning with his hair still wet and sticking straight up on top. "You look like a rooster," laughed Patsy. And that was it, *placa* for life.

Ray was always "Raydog" and nobody knew where that came from.

For eight years they've been good friends and homeboys in the bustling barrio by Our Lady of Guadalupe Church, where neighbors are endlessly chatting and kids are dodging cars in the street as the Eastern Cities Transit bus slices right down the middle, drowning out conversations and choking everyone with clouds of smoky exhaust.

Little Rooster had been complaining about headaches but it wasn't until he almost fainted on the way to holy communion that his mom and dad began to worry. After a few visits to the Belvedere clinic, his parents decided to send him to the county general hospital for more tests and evaluations.

Two weeks later, during one of his many trips to the hospital's third floor, Ray is walking down the corridor to room 406 with a green chile burrito stashed in his jacket. The burrito is for the Roosterman. He glances through the wire-meshed glass window into the waiting room and notices at least fifteen Avilas, some pacing, some sitting and wringing their hands.

Ray almost bumps into a nurse as he enters the room, the smell of disinfectant biting at his nose. Little Rooster is lying on the bed, IVs plugged into his arm and an oxygen tube strapped to his nose, with his head buzzed to just a stubble, one side shaved clean.

"Hey, Roost, you look like a bionic cholo lying there," says Ray nervously.

"Raydog, what's up?" Little Rooster's voice is soft, just above a whisper, his eyes aimlessly searching for Ray.

"I brought you a burrito from Garduno's 'cause I know the food here..."

Rooster interrupts. "They're gonna take this thing outta my head, but they don't know."

"What do you mean, bro? You're gonna be fine."

"They don't know what's gonna happen."

"What's going to happen is that the docs are gonna fix you up and you're gonna get out of here and everything will be fine and good."

Ray's heart is in his throat, the words coming out in small chunks. He begins to cry.

Ray grabs his hand and squeezes hard.

"Don't disappear, damn it, don't disappear – what am I gonna do without you?"

Suddenly the room becomes hushed, the buzz and hum of the medical equipment seems transformed into music, low and comforting.

"I won't disappear, I'll never go away."

"I love you, Homes. Shit, I can't even say that to my pop," says Ray.

Rooster's grip on Ray's hand loosens, his eyes appear to be looking right through Ray.

Little Rooster smiles, "I love you too."

Ray's tennis shoes stick to the hot asphalt as he walks across the parking lot toward the bus stop on State Street and Marengo. Ha! The green burrito is still stuffed in his jacket pocket. When he gets to the corner, he looks up at the palm trees moving slowly in the warm wind. He straightens up his back and stares at the street sign, not exactly sure how he got there.

"Hey, bud, come on, can you help a guy out?" A homeless man is holding his hand out to Ray Dog. Ray pulls the foil-wrapped burrito out of his jacket pocket and drops it into the old guy's hand.

"That's from the Roosterman," says Ray.

three

SOMETHING CALLED LOVE

EMILY

■ A DREAM MAY ESCAPE BUT A MEMORY IS FOREVER.

Emily, take me across the water home
Emily, look how much we have grown
Emily, I still remember the day
Waking up, chasing the shadows away
It won't be long until I see your face
Eyes as bright as the sun
It won't be far down this lonesome road
Until I see you again

Emily, run so fast through the fields
Make believe all our dreams were so real

It won't be long until I see you smile
Turning my night into day
It won't be far down this lonely way
Until I can hold you again

Emily, we can hide, hide from them all
Emily, they can't catch us
They can't catch us now
They can't catch us now

TAKE MY HAND

■ WHEN TRUE LOVE IS HIDING IN PLAIN SIGHT.

Girl, you know you can't go on this way
Night after night day after every day
Whisper to me what's in your aching heart
This love you need is not very far

Baby, dry the tears from your eyes
And take my hand as we walk into the night

A soul on fire and a touch that's cold
Seems to me that's all you've ever known
Desperately looking for something that's real
Hard to find is the love that can heal

Tender are the dreams
That we try so hard to hide, so deep inside

I don't know why you go on this way
Night after night and about every day
Tell to me the secrets only a girl could know
How much to feel and just how much to show

Baby, dry the tears from your eyes
And take my hand as we walk into the night

LUZ DE MI VIDA

■ WE WILL ALWAYS BE JUNTOS, OKAY?

Cuando you and me
We were just *chiquillos*
We would always run
Through the tall *nopal*
We would often say
Say to each other
There could be no *fin*
Siempre los dos

Luz de mi vida
Eres la voz de mi son
You are forever
Light of my *corazón*

It was *en la mañana*
In our *rinconcito*
Was the time you played me
Sang me your *canción*
Pues when I heard your voice
Y tu melodía
You so touched my heart
And so moved my soul

Luz de mi vida
Eres la voz de mi son
You are forever
Light of my *corazón*

I remember everything as you
And in all the things that I do
And *en the calle y en el cuartel*
Me recuerdo de tu querer

Luz de mi vida
Eres la voz de mi son

I remember everything as you
And in all the things that I do
And *en* the *calle y en el cuartel*
Me recuerdo de tu querer

CURE FOR LOVE

■ THE PRESCRIPTION IS WRITTEN
IN DISAPPEARING INK.

You bring me roses
You give me kisses
You bring me moons and stars
That shine so high up in the sky
My heart is beating wild and crazy
Hope that I can find
A cure for love

Could be you want me
Could be you care
Could be the words you say
Are things I just want to hear
You got me nervous, got me shaking
Maybe I can find
A cure for love

When the phone rings
No one answers
The letters come back saying
"Lover cannot be found"
Don't go looking, don't bother searching
You see it's because she
Found herself a cure for love

LA PISTOLA Y EL CORAZÓN

■ A MEXICAN COWBOY MOVIE WITH OUR
SAD HERO RIDING OFF INTO THE SUNSET.

No se como decirte
No se como explicarte
Que aquí no hay remedio
De lo que siento yo
De lo que siento yo

La luna me dice una cosa
Las estrellas me dicen otra
Y la luz del día me canta
Esta triste canción
Esta triste canción

No se como amarte
No se como abrasarte
Porque no se me deja
Este dolor que tengo yo
El dolor que tengo yo

Esta noche tan oscura con sus
Sombras tan tranquilas
Y el viento me sigue cantando
Esta humilde canción
Esta humilde canción

Los besos que me diste mi amor
Son los que me están matando
Ya las lágrimas me están secando
Con mi pistola y mi corazón
Y aquí siempre paso la vida con
La pistola y el corazón

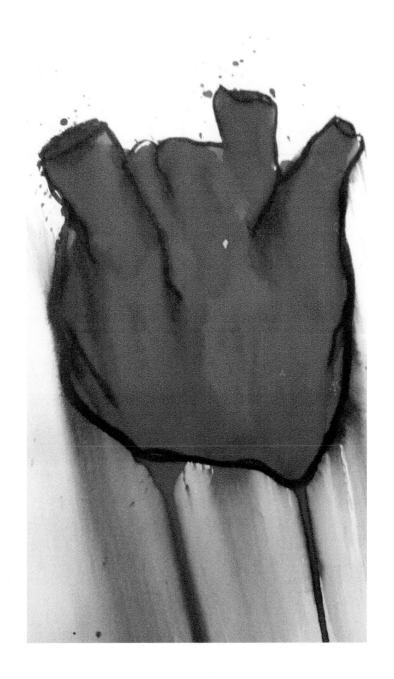

CHAINS OF LOVE

■ A BIG CHAIN AND A SMALL VERY SMALL HACKSAW.

I'm a prisoner here
By your design
And the key to the door
Oh I can't find

Closing in here
Are these four walls
Not even a dime will you give me
To make my one call

I don't know
What a man is supposed to do
When the joy is gone
Gone away from you

Ain't no hammer, ain't no rock
Can break the lock on these chains
These chains of love

I drag down the boulevard
This ball of steel
And the ties that bind me
Are all too real

I got to go free
Like a bird up in the air
Like a child in the schoolyard
Without a care

Ain't no hammer, ain't no rock
Can break the lock on these chains

Ain't no spell, none I can tell
Can take away these chains
Ain't no how to get out
Out of these chains of love
These chains of love

Look at the clock
So much time
I look again
And the hands are stopped

Ain't no hammer, ain't no rock
Can break the lock on these chains
Ain't no spell none I can tell
Can take away these chains
These chains of love

HEARTS OF STONE

I travel down this lonely road
To see if I can pick me a rose
But all I find is a handful of thorns
In a place where blossoms grow

Some hearts are made of stone
Some are cold, made of ice
Some beat all alone
Then there are those made of steel
Ones that don't even feel
Where are those hearts?
Those hearts made of gold

I wandered down this lonely trail
Some twenty seven hours a day
But all I see are footprints in the dirt
Where others tried to find their way

How far will I go
To leave these fears behind
Let those tears go dry
Won't stop until I can find
That heart of gold

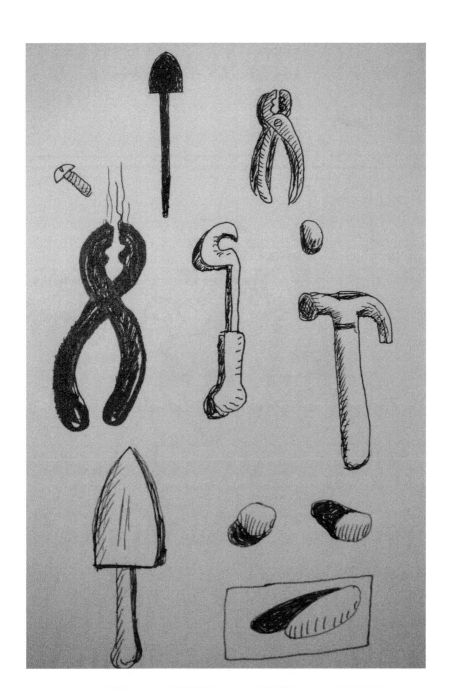

WHAT GOOD IS LOVE

■ Nobody's been able to figure it out yet.

What good is time
What good is time if it isn't spent with you

What good is the sun
What good is the sun if it can't shine on you

What good is love
What good is love if we can't say it's true

She has a restless soul
And she doesn't even know

I ask the moon and the stars
I ask the moon and the stars to watch over you

This train keeps rolling, now at quarter past two
Taking his broken heart back to you

TIN CAN TRUST

■ PENNIES AND LOVE IN A COFFEE CAN UNDER THE BED.

I don't look
It don't look like I'm going nowhere
Five cents for a bottle
A quarter rolling down the stairs
All in all I ain't got
Ain't got much in a tin can trust

Don't know how
But it's gotta be going somewhere
A dime store shirt
And two bucks for a good pair
All in all it ain't much
Ain't got much in a tin can trust

Little darling
I can't buy you
Those golden rings and things
But, honey
I can give you
One thing a man can bring

All in all I ain't got
Don't got much
All in all there ain't much
Just some love in a tin can trust

Oh, darling
Can't buy you
All those pretty things
Fancy cars and diamond rings
Oh, honey
Got nothin'
It's only love I bring

BIG AUGUST MOON

■ DO WE EVER GET BACK WHAT WE LOST?

Big August moon
The years go by too soon
They're all gone
But I'm still here
And I know it'll never be that way again

Hands holding tight
Loving with all our might
But now you're gone
And I'm still here
And I know it'll never be that way again

Here I stand alone
Solid as a stone
But a stone also crumbles
And I hope it could be that way again

Big August moon
The years go by too soon
I can't say
If I'll be here
But I know it'll never be that way again

four

GOOD MORNING AZTLAN

MÁS Y MÁS

■ ANY FRIDAY NIGHT IN THE BARRIO OF MAKE BELIEVE.

Let's go, *mi chula*
Come on out with me
We can throw a *chancla*
Until half *pasado de* three
Get all tangled up
Fall on the floor
Go out, *bailando*
Beat down all the doors

Uno pa delante
Otro pa detrás
Dame chispas, baby
Dame más y más y más y más

Let's go, *bailando*
Noche is looking fine
Jump into the *carro*
Drink a bunch of wine
Don't tell us nothing
We look outta sight
Tell a lotta lies and
Go outside and fight

Uno pa delante
Otro pa detras
Dame chispas, honey
Dame más y más y más y más

VIKING

■ HE WAS A *BATO* LIKE ANY OTHER *BATO*.

The last time I seen Viking
He was about this tall
With a tattoo
Where a smile should've been
Of his sweetheart's name
Of his sweetheart's name

Do you remember Viking?
He was just like you and me
With a big scar
Where his heart should've been
Inside his chest
Inside his chest

Do you remember Viking?
Do you remember Viking?

The last time I saw Viking
He was about so tall
With a tattoo
Where his heart should've been
He was about everything
He was about everything
Do you remember Viking?
I remember Viking

THE HARDEST TIME

■ SHE EARNED EVERY GRAY HAIR ON HER 18-YEAR-OLD HEAD.

A toast to love with paper cups
And a vow to never part
They're saying to each other there's a fire burning
Deep within their hearts
But at her darkest hour he's gone far away
She's all alone
And when the lights go out it's the hardest time
The hardest time to be alone

She sends her Mary off to school
And sits to watch TV
They're talking about spending their lives together
The way it's supposed to be
Then the baby cries, wakes her from her dream
She's on her own
And when the lights go out it's the hardest time
The hardest time to be alone

A mother's dream is like a story never told
Reaching out for something more than a hand to hold
Wanting the girl she left behind
So far behind

Pen and paper in her hand
To write the folks back home
She's telling them again that her life is better
Not like long ago
Then her shaking hand tears across the page
As it crumbles to the floor

And when the lights go out it's the hardest time
The hardest time to be alone

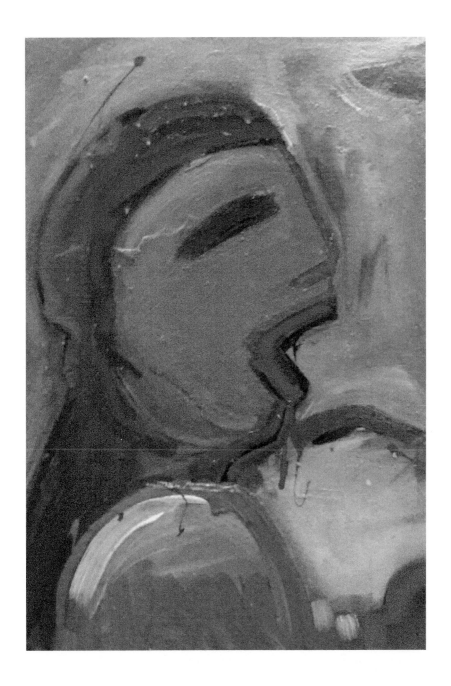

IRONSIDES

■ LOAD UP THE TRUCK, LUPE, WE'RE GOING TO THE DRIVE-IN MOVIES!

Pues vamonos entonces, we'll take Ironsides
Ay papá, do we have to take the truck?
Why not, *mi hija*? You can sit in back and watch the movie
What if it gets cold? Come on, put a jacket then and hurry up

Mom, can't we take Lily's Celica? We can all fit
Look *mi hija*, that's your padre and he likes doing stuff like that
But, Ma, I don't—especially when he drops me off at school
It's embarrassing
I could go to school with Lily
Or I could always walk, it's not that far—right, Rudy?
Get off Dad's case, *moco*, he's *ruco*
That's his *troca*, what do ya want?

Don't call me that, you stupid—I'm just saying…
I am now announcing that Ironsides is now ready for boarding
for our trip to the movie show
Starring Ricardo Montalban and some *gueras*!

We squeezed into the cab
Picked up Mama Lisa
Stopped to get some sodas
And drove off to the show

CUCA'S BLUES

I remember Cuca
With red lips and ink black hair
In the picture that I found

I can see her dancing
When the music was low and slow
In shiny dress and jewelry
Somewhere they used to go

That was so long ago
When the Red Car would always ride
Way on up to Spring Street
Down the tracks to the other side

They pulled over and dropped her
At the house so late at night
She waved her keys and said goodbye
And went inside to cry

I guess she had some babies
And two more after that
They grew up men and ladies
And some got old and fat

She got a call from Tony
"What happened yesterday
When a man came down to see you?"
She didn't have much to say

LATIN TRIP

■ DON'T ASK NO QUESTIONS, JUST REMEMBER THIS FACE

Don't go figure
It's not about hip
You won't get it
It's a Latin trip

Low note rumble
Go so high
Roll so slow
Just passing by

Dark eyes looking
Headlight flash
Loop down around
Right on back

Top slick straight
Crease done right
Shades put on
In black midnight

Downtown cool
And uptown talk
Bad boy look
And magic walk

Don't go figure
It's not about hip
You won't get it
It's a Latin trip

GOOD MORNING, AZTLÁN

■ LET'S WAKE UP, EAST L.A.

There's a tattoo heart
With an arrow through the middle
Of a name that looks like Joe
And a young girl is looking
At her makeup in the mirror
Puts a little gold ring on her toe

I've got to say one, two
Three more things before I go on

There is a sharp dressed man
Playing something on a fiddle
In the backyard right next door
And everybody's mother
Is cooking something in the kitchen
Got dishes stacked from ceiling to floor

I've got to say one, two
Three more things before I go on

You can't run and try to hide away
Here it comes, here comes another day

A red rooster crows
A little Mexican tune
On the chain link fence by the gate
Somebody's daddy out there
Honking on the horn
Hurry up, we're going to make him late

I've got to say one, two
Three more things before I go on

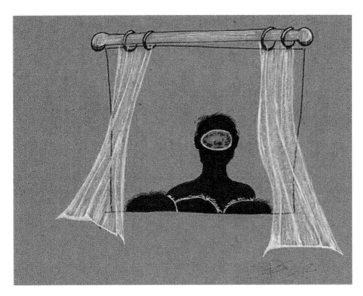

You can't run and try to hide away
Here it comes, here comes another day

If you're long down that highway
No matter where you are
You're never really far
Good morning, Aztlán

There's a big fat heart
With an arrow through the middle
Of this place that I call home
And when I get lost
And don't even have a nickel
There is a piece of dirt I can call my own

I've got to say one, two
Three more things before I go on

You can't run and try to hide away
Here it comes, here comes another day
Where you are, never really far away
Good morning, Aztlán

PALETERO

■ I SWEAR, HOMES, HE EVEN HAD AVOCADO FLAVOR ONCE!

Yo soy un paletero
Y te vengo a vender
Unas ricas paletitas
El sabor que gusta usted

Aquí tengo de aguacate
Tambien tengo de limón
Yo traigo de naranja
Y hasta tengo de jamón

Tengo fresa, uva, pasa
O el sabor que quieres tu
Si te gusta algo que pica
Hasta tengo chile, too

Yo soy un paletero
Y no se a donde voy
Pero vendo alegría
Y un paletero soy, okay!

I got all kind of colors
Like these green and white and red
And if you do not like it
Try a purple one instead

You'll like them in the summer
When the *sol* is really hot
And even in the winter
Whether it is cold or not

I can sell them for a quarter
Or I can sell them for a dime

I've got some that taste like whiskey
And some as sweet as wine

I am a *paletero*
And I don't know where I go
But I can sell you something happy
Because *un paletero* knows, okay!

ON MAIN STREET

■ Any Saturday afternoon in the 'hood.

Nothing better than walking down the boulevard
Feeling the sun on my face
Watching Maggie and Connie with their little kids
Running around all over the place

Got a red light
Got a green light
Don't matter which way I go
Down main street
Down easy street
It's when I feel like I'm home

Nothing better than strolling down the boulevard
With a little time on my side
All worries gone away to somewhere else
With only a blink of an eye

Got a red light
Got a green light
Don't matter which way I go

Going home
The only place I know
Take me there
Where the days go slow

Nothing better than running down the boulevard
Getting a little dirt on my shoes
With my brothers and sisters hanging all around
Chasing away all of my blues

THE NEIGHBORHOOD

■ A BARRIO'S DREAMS AND WISHES.

Brother finds trouble on the street
A piece of rock to make men weak
Trembling eyes at everyone he meets

Sister holds her baby in the bed
Dreams and wishes dancing in her head
A love forever is what he said—that's what he said

Father leans back in his easy chair
A pint of whiskey—he just sits and stares
He don't know and he doesn't really care

Mother works at her nine-to-five
Hardly makes enough to keep alive
She bows her head with tears in her eyes

They're just songs sung on a dirty street
Echoes of hope lie beneath their feet
Struggling hard to make ends meet

Thank you Lord for another day
Help my brother along his way
And please bring peace to the neighborhood
Grant us all peace and serenity

ANGELS WITH DIRTY FACES

■ HOMELESS IN THE CITY OF THE ANGELS.

Broken window smile
Weeds for hair
Strolling around the corner
Like a millionaire

And the angels with dirty faces
Go it alone

With one shoe on
And one shoe lost
Stands a wounded man
Who just laughs it off

And the angels with dirty faces
Go it alone

Lost a brother last night
To the howling wind
Find an empty doorway
It'll be back again

And the angels with dirty faces
Go it alone.

ONE TIME ONE NIGHT

■ QUIET VOICES WHISPER STORIES OF AMERICA.

A wise man was telling stories to me
About the places he had been to
And the things that he had seen

A lady dressed in white with the man she loved
Standing along the side of their pickup truck
A shot rang out in the night
Just when everything seemed right
Another headline written down in America

The guy that lived next door in 305
Took the kids to the park and disappeared
About half past nine
Who will ever know
How much she loved them so
That dark night alone in America

A quiet voice is singing something to me
An age-old song about the home of the brave
In this land here of the free
One time one night in America

Four small boys playing ball in a parking lot
A preacher, a teacher and the other became a cop
A car skidded in the rain
Making the last little one a saint
One more light goes out in America

A young girl tosses a coin in the wishing well
She hopes for a heaven while for her
There's just this hell
She gave away her life
To become somebody's wife
Another wish unanswered in America

People having so much faith
Die too soon while all the rest come late
We write a song that no one sings
On a cold black stone
Where a lasting peace will finally bring

The sunlight plays upon my windowpane
I wake up to a world that's still the same
My father said to be strong
And that a good man could never do wrong
In a dream I had last night in America

A wise man was telling stories to me
About the places he had been to
And the things that he had seen

A quiet voice is singing something to me
An age-old song about the home of the brave
In this land here of the free
One time one night in America

THE CITY

■ ALL THAT GLITTERS IS THE CITY.

Come on, let's go out tonight
Out into the neon light
Sidewalk shining from the rain
From First and Hill to Sixth and Main

Two lovers kissing by the door
There's yelling from the second floor

Come on, let's go, let's go get high
Out into the neon night
Hit every spot along the way
From Paramount to Cudahy

A man is calling out a name
A rose wrapped up in cellophane

Come on, let's fall down tonight
Shoot out all the neon lights
People dancing real slow
The music plays until the rooster crows

THE TOWN

■ THE TOWN IS WHERE YOUR SOUL CAN BE FOUND.

A car rolls by way down low
There's a name on a wall that I know
I heard a shot go off in the night
My father said everything is all right
In the town where I come from

Some kids are playing out in the yard
A mother says, "Don't wander too far"
I can go there when I dream
I close my eyes and it's all I see
The town where I come from

I know it's where my heart will be found
It's where I'll finally lay myself down
I can go there when I dream
I close my eyes and it's all I see
The town where I come from

IN 1964

■ IN 1964, YOU COULD SEE THE SEARS TOWER ON OLYMPIC BOULEVARD FROM ANYWHERE IN EAST L.A.

It stood guardian-like over rivers of concrete that pointed eastward toward Boyle Heights, and the then-green hills of City Terrace

Crayola-colored stucco houses where mexicanos took their residence long ago ran up those hills

Behind flapping screen doors a million moms rolled buttered tortillas and gave Kool-Aid to their kids as they ran out the door to play in the dust

We chased watermelon trucks in the summertime or rode the Kern bus for a dime to the Chicano Miracle Mile, Whittier Boulevard, to watch movies at the Boulevard Theater

We saw the "Three Stooges in Orbit" there, on the screen Moe hit Larry, in the lobby Lencho hit Rudy and we all ran out to squint into the sun

We'd lie on the convertible sofa on hot nights with the door wide open to catch a breeze and hear dad's same old stories about the war, monsters, and uncle Manuel's operation to remove a splinter that grew to the size of a small tree

Every mother's day he'd buy mom these sweaters that she'd rewrap and put away, just to keep wearing the tattered orange one she wore on her migration from Colorado to L.A. in 1922

My Grandma Cuca didn't speak any English, so she'd sit and watch TV with the sound turned down and make up her own plots, her best friend was a guy she called "Gunsmoke"

Life never seemed or wanted to change in that little white house on

Hammel Street, with its decorative iron and mosaic of plant pots sitting on the porch rails

There was always this thing about East L.A., born of the earth and risen up, not unlike the San Gabriels we'd occasionally see when the wind blew the smog down through the valley, surrounding us in the mystery of who we were and where we'd come from

It was something that we couldn't see, but we could feel, something that we couldn't hear but resonated in our bones

And in the roses and rosaries and the damp smell of beans boiling, a sad happy forever spun all around us and held us to its breast

So click your heels all you want Dolores, you can never go home, but sometimes you can strip it all away, make it all go away

And in that only-free-place of paled memory, in that oneness of Space, Time and Spirit, we tumble naked through the universe back into those warm sweatered arms again, it's then we can all go home

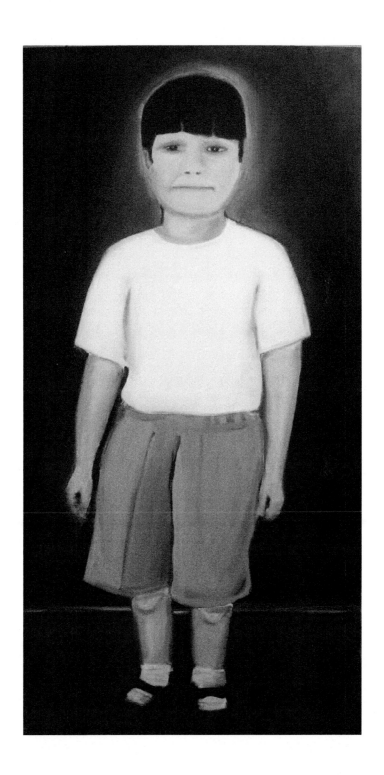

five

JOURNEYS

WAKE UP DOLORES

■ A MAGICAL TRIP BACK HOME.

My legs are tired
My face feels hot
Wake up Dolores
Please try to walk

Oh sacred night
Ocuiltin
Moyacatla

Our light is dim
We have so far to go
The stones are hard
On this endless road

Oh sacred night
On quetzal plumes
Of dying suns
And purple moons
Oh sacred night

As an eagle soars
Our spirits fly
To our gentle rest
Under loving sky

Oh sacred night
On quetzal plumes
Of dying suns
And purple moons
Oh sacred night

GATES OF GOLD

■ WHEN YOU'RE NEARING THE END OF THE ROAD, YOU WONDER WHAT YOU SHOULD DO WITH THE TIME YOU HAVE LEFT. BEYOND THOSE HILLS WE FIND THE REST OF OUR LIVES.

Far away beyond those hills is mystery untold
Far off almost out of sight there's beauty to behold
Which way do we go, can't say that I know

Some say it's a place where you'll never grow old
Lord knows what we'll find behind those gates of gold

Almost there and yet so far is where we'll find our home
So close but still so far are stories to be told
Which way do we go, can't say that I know

Some say it's a place where you'll never grow old
Lord knows what we'll find behind those gates of gold

Mama, come gently rock my soul
And tell me please, what we'll find behind those gates of gold

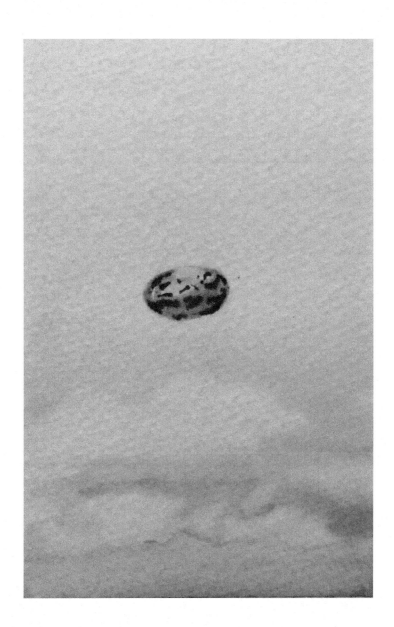

EVERYBODY LOVES A TRAIN

■ THEY MAY CALL US INSANE BUT WE JUST LOVE THAT CRAZY TRAIN.

A long time done away on Eastside, Southside,
Los Angeles, Detroit, America, U.S.A.
Sittin' right about here watchin' high heels
And sneakers tread concrete platform
Headin' straight for who-knows-where
And why and how come

Clack, clack, clack
Goin' down the rails and comin' back
Train a-comin' n goin'
Clack, clack, clack
Clack, clack, clack

I'm thinkin' in sick brain,
"Say man, where you goin'
With all those stories wrapped up in suitcase
And handbags and old rags?"
Says, "I can't say, but the 12:40's got my name."
Well it goes without sayin'
Everybody loves a train

Steel whistle blowin' a crazy sound
Jump on a car when she comes around
Steel whistle blowin' a crazy sound
Jump on a car when she comes around

Clack, clack, clack
Goin' down the rails and comin' back
Train a-comin' n goin'
Clack, clack, clack
Clack, clack, clack

Just goes without saying
That everybody loves a train
Go ahead and call us insane
But we all just love a train

TONY AND MARÍA

■ A TRUE STORY.

One-hundred and fifty miles from Mexico to L.A.
Doesn't seem that far but still a world away
Went up to see her husband Tony
Who left some years ago
He wrote to say come be with me
I love and miss you so

"And I promise that I'll care for you,"
Wrote Tony to his wife
"Now and for the rest of my life"

Tony washes dishes, María she sweeps floors
The dreams that they once had
Well, they don't have them anymore
Instead, she stares up at the ceiling
While most are fast asleep
She thinks about her babies
And prays the Lord their souls to keep

"We promised that we'd care for them,"
Said Tony to his wife
"Now and for the rest of our lives"

One time late at night while looking at the sky
They saw a shooting star
Burning silver and so bright
They said could this here be a sign
That it's time to go back home
Because even with you near me
I still feel so all alone

"We promised that we'd care for one another,"
Said his wife
"Now and for the rest of our lives"

RIVER OF FOOLS

■ LIVES ARE LIKE RIVERS.

Memories of a lonely past
A boat sailed into the wind
Drifting lost in waters of doubt
On a journey that has no end

Torn and faded photographs
A chest full of old goodbyes
Tear-streaked faces by the light of the moon
Here on a river of fools
Here on a river of fools

A trio of angels holding candles of light
Guide the ship to an unknown shore
Sad soul riders with arms drawn tight
As they stopped for just one more

Fingers pointed to a star in the sky
A message from someone they can't see
Tear-streaked faces by the light of the moon
Here on a river of fools
Here on a river of fools

Traveling along a cloudy path
With a wing, a heart and a prayer
Pieces fall from the heavens above
To a place they know not where

A string of beads in trembling hands
Heading close to the judgment day
Tear-streaked faces by the light of the moon
Here on a river of fools
Here on a river of fools

THE ROAD TO GILA BEND

■ ALWAYS RUNNING, ALWAYS RUNNING.

Made Nogales overnight
Through the desert in the yellow light
Missing everything I left behind
Will they see me coming
Do they know I'm running?

Got to Tucson in the dark
Keeping an eye out for the law
Five-hundred miles or more from a broken heart
Can they see me coming?

It's a long, long way to Gila Bend
One silver dollar in my hand
The road twists and turns—is there no end?
When I get there I can lay my head in Gila Bend

Saw a church along the way
A place to hide, to kneel and pray
Help me make it maybe one more day
Can they see me coming?

It's a long, long way to Gila Bend
One silver dollar in my hand
The road twists and turns—is there no end?
When I get there I can lay my head in Gila Bend

WHISKEY TRAIL

■ THAT ENDLESS ROAD OF WINE AND WHISKEY.

Heaven is a place where good men go
Maybe it's a place that I won't know
Heading down that whiskey trail

Mama told me not to run, because I might fall
But I never was the kind to listen much at all
Heading down that whiskey trail

Daddy drank his dinner from a paper sack
Made it out the door one day
And he never came back
Heading down that whiskey trail

They say that I'm a chip off a son of a gun
With nowhere to hide out and nowhere to run
Heading down that whiskey trail

Can't you hear the engines wail?
Damn that old whiskey trail

THE VALLEY

■ THE FOOD ON OUR TABLE FROM THE WORK OF HUMAN HANDS.

In ancient times to a place so far away
Across the land where the earth was as tough as clay
Looked at their hands, looked all around
And they seemed pleased at what they had found

Here in the valley, bread on the table
Work through day hard for as long as we are able
Green is the valley, blue is the night
Out of the shadows, into the light

They could've gone but instead they chose to stay
To watch the clouds way up high as they turned to gray
Then through the dark, broke a crimson sun
And at that moment, they knew their lives had just begun

Here in the valley, bread on the table
Work through day hard for as long as we are able
Green is the valley, blue is the night
Out of the darkness, into the light

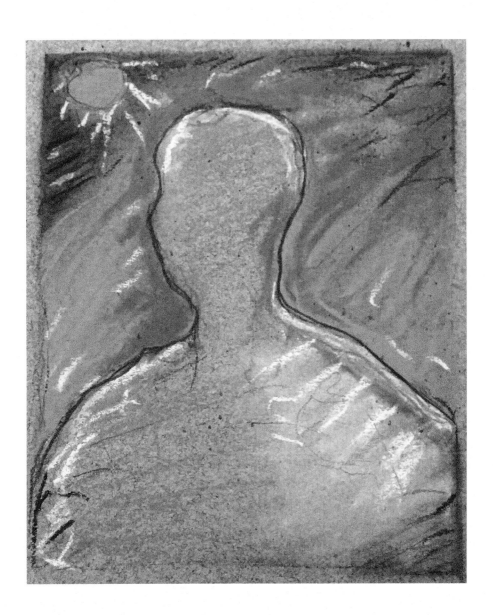

135

A MATTER OF TIME

Speak softly, don't wake the baby
Come and hold me once more
Before I have to leave
I hear there's a lot of work out there
Everything will be fine
And I'll send for you, baby
Just a matter of time

Hard life, the only thing we know
Come and tell me once more
Before you have to go
That there's a better world out there
Though it don't feel right
Will it be like our home
Just a matter of time

And I hope it's all it seems
Not another empty dream
There's a time for you and me
In a place living happily

And I hope it's all that it seems
Not another empty dream
There's a time for you and me
In a place living happily

Walk quietly, don't make a sound
Believe in what you're doing
I know we can't be wrong
Don't worry about us here
It will be all right

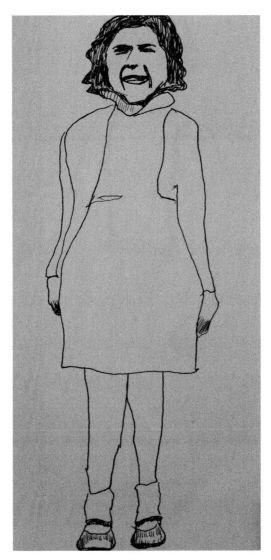

And we'll be there with you
Just a matter of time

And we'll all be together
Just a matter of time

THE WRECK OF THE CARLOS REY

■ SHIPWRECKS AND HEARTBREAK.

Fifty traveling to work the fields
Toil the factories and sweat the steel

Set out to sail from Santa Rosalía
I left you a note tacked to a tree

Adiós querida
I'll return one day
Now I'm leaving on the Carlos Rey

Four cruel days under stormy skies
Not much bread to keep us alive

The wind kicked up and the rain came down
Then we all heard a terrible sound

Adiós querida
Nothing more to say
I'm lost in the wreck of the Carlos Rey

I struggled against the pull of the tide
I clutched my bag with your picture inside

But my heart did break as it slipped away
Disappearing into the gray

Adiós querida
I've gone to stay
Down in the wreck of the Carlos Rey

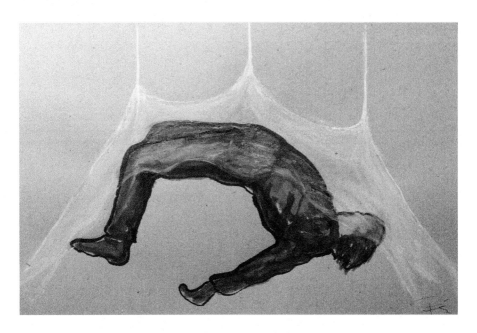

In the dark and cold I let you go
With the hunk of wood that I took hold

I sleep in a bed of salt and sand
And dream sweet dreams of taking your hand

Adiós querida
I'm gone away
Down in the wreck of the Carlos Rey

27 SPANISHES

■ THE STORY OF THE CONQUEST OF MEXICO
IN 4 MINUTES AND 38 SECONDS.

Twenty-seven Spanishes
Arriving from the sea
Blades of steel flashing
Cutting down the eagle's tree

Came riding in on mountains
On red and silver steeds
Into the city of the serpent
Through the gates of the Otomí

A soldier dressed in iron asks
Where do you all come from?
From the earth of four directions
From the purple clouds above

Just then a rain came falling down
As the wind began to blow
The sky then turned to crimson
With a sound so deep and low

Said the brown prince to the Spanishes
As he raised a mighty hand:
Don't come here bringing worries
To the people of this land

Their swords then turned to deadly snakes
Like the ones found in the grass
Get back into those silly ships
Before we kick your ass

But the strangers made an offer
So the Brown Prince said, "Why not"

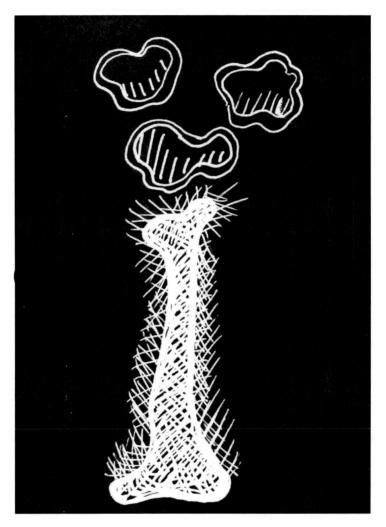

And they ended up with empty plates
And boot soup in a pot

Later they became *muy* friendly
And their blood was often mixed
Now they all hang out together
And play guitars for kicks

THE LONG GOODBYE

■ WE SPEND OUR LIVES SAYING GOODBYE.

When we were children and the first school bell rang
The kids did hurry as the birds all sang
We looked at our mothers as tears filled her eyes
And you know it's a long goodbye

The day he first saw her he said she's the one
The skies then opened because the searching was done
Then she was gone with a blink of an eye
And you know it's a long goodbye

Spinning and spinning the world like a top
The wheels keeps turning seem never to stop
All of a sudden rain falls from the sky and she cries
It's a long goodbye

She knew he was all right the last time he wrote
He sent some money because she was so broke
But soon came a letter with a medal inside
And she knows it's a long goodbye

When I got home there were lights on the tree
The kids all stood up they were waiting for me
But again I woke up with a prayer and a sigh
And you know it's a long goodbye

Spinning and spinning the world like a top
The wheels keeps turning seem never to stop
All of a sudden rain falls from the sky and she cries
It's a long goodbye

HOLY HELL

■ IF LIFE GIVES YOU LEMONS... BUY TEQUILA.

"Where the hell do you think you're going?" Carlos asks himself as he eyeballs the pile of black trash bags stacked so high on the back seat that they almost block out his view through the rear window. "Is it too late to go back? Maybe I can tell them I was just kidding, that I didn't mean anything I said." It was the eighteenth time he'd asked himself that question in a hundred and seventy-five miles, which comes to roughly once every nine miles — but who's counting?

Carlos kept talking to himself. It took seventeen years to get me where I am now, behind the wheel of my old man's 1990 Oldsmobile Cutlass Sierra station wagon, considered a classic by two people in Tulsa. The clock on the dashboard says 6:47 am. My dad should be finding his car missing any minute now. I'm such a big boy now aren't I, Pop?
A little bit of sun is winking on the horizon, it won't be long before it's 1,000 degrees on this miserable desert road. My only companion is this Spanish talk radio guy on the one station this crap car radio can get. I should be fluent by the time I get to Tucson.

I guess I got nothing to complain about and about everything to whine about. I'm a living, breathing, healthy human even though somewhat incomplete. I lost my left foot in a weird Ferris wheel accident at eight years old when Artie Nuñez enthusiastically rocked the wheel car too close to the guide wire. That's where my bitching started. As a kid I got called by every nickname you can imagine, from kickstand to flat tire. I cheerfully let it roll off me while I killed them all in my mind.

Looking at the outline of some hills way off in the distance as the sky goes from deep purple to pale blue, I'm beginning to think that this trip is more like an exercise than an exorcism. That, even if shit gets too much, there will always be plenty more where that came from and if kindness cannot be found, it's got to be created and if life gives you lemons... buy tequila.

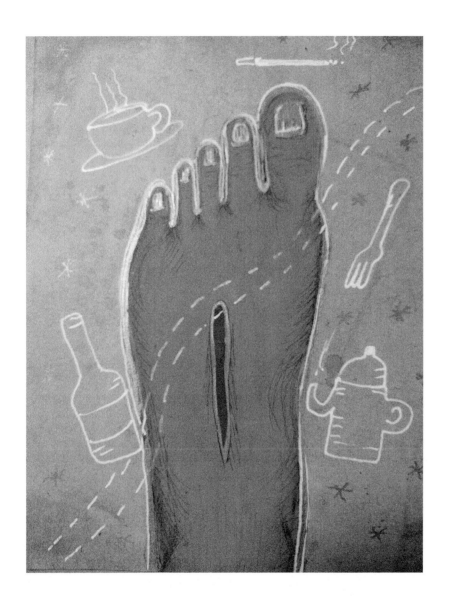

SIX

TRUTH & PASSION

WILL THE WOLF SURVIVE?

■ AN ANTHEM, A MANTRA, A SONG ABOUT DETERMINATION.

Through the chill of winter
Running across a frozen lake
Hunters are out on his trail
All odds are against him
With a family to provide for
The one thing he must keep alive
Will the wolf survive?

Drifting by the roadside
Lines etched on an aging face
Wants to make some honest pay
Losing to the range war
He's got two strong legs to guide him
Two strong arms keep him alive
Will the wolf survive?

Standing in the pouring rain
All alone in a world that's changed
Running scared, now forced to hide
In a land where he once stood with pride
But he'll find his way by the morning light

Sounds across the nation
Coming from young hearts and minds
Battered drums and old guitars
Singing songs of passion
It's the truth that they all look for
The one thing they must keep alive
Will the wolf survive

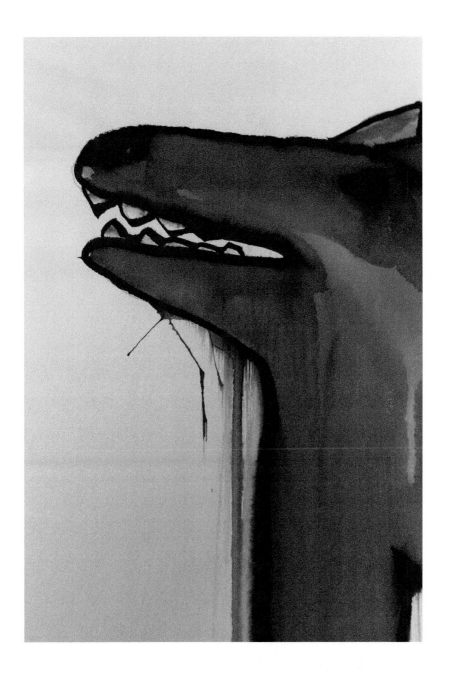

REVOLUTION

■ AN OLD RADICAL RECALLS HIS REBEL HEART.

Where did it go?
Can't say that I know
Those times of revolution
Of burnin', burnin', burnin'
All so cool and gone
What was, just was

We tried, my brother,
To hold on to our fate
Or was it too late for revolution?
Too tired, too tired, sister
To hold my fist so high
Now that it's gone

Too tired brother, sister
To hold my fist so high
Now that it's gone
Gone away

Where did it go?
Can we say we know?
Those times of revolution
Our time of revolution

BURN IT DOWN

■ IF YOU CAN'T BEAT 'EM, BURN 'EM.

I didn't say a word
It's only destiny I've heard
The time had come for me to run away
Don't even turn around is what they say

I couldn't say a word
It's only dignity I've heard
But once I go, there is no coming back
Throw away all that I once had

I'll burn it down
Gonna burn it down
Gonna burn it down

Had tied me up and I couldn't breathe
I cut the rope and then I broke free
Whatever was left I threw it down into the dirt
And kicked the dust until my damned eyes hurt

I'll burn it down
Gonna burn it down
Gonna burn it all down

I couldn't say one word
It's just mystery I heard
Maybe I'll miss it on some lonely day
And maybe think about what I might say

I'll burn it down
Until it's gone, gone, gone
Gonna burn it all down

WHAT IN THE WORLD

■ LET'S ALL RUN OUT AND HAVE A NICE LIFE.

When we don't seem to see eye-to-eye
Our arms reach out to ask but why
You're not alone, call me on the phone
And tell me, oh tell me
Oh what in the world
What in the world will we do

When a house of cards comes tumbling down
And the pieces lie there on the ground
Don't be afraid, it can't be too late
Tell me, oh tell me
Oh what in the world
What in the world will we do

When a bird flies high up in the sky
Funny how we sit and wonder why
Suppose that we could be that free
Tell me, oh tell me
Oh what in the world
What in the world will we do

When a bird flies high up in the sky
It's funny how we sit and wonder why
Suppose that we could be that free
Suppose you and me
Were always that free
Imagine, imagine
Oh what this world
What this world could be

THE MESS WE'RE IN

■ MAYBE WE SHOULD BE LIKE JANITORS AND SWEEP UP THE CIGARETTE BUTTS OF THE WORLD.

We've got no money
But we've got our lives
A voice that's louder than any picket sign
Don't take away what is ours to keep
This very land that lies beneath our feet
Don't know about this mess we're in
Bombs are bursting in a far-off land

Fire in the sky, a soldier takes his stand
But who is to know about the rules that men make
For what honor and for whose sake
Don't know about this mess we're in

The smoke is clearing and we see a light
Coming together for a different fight
All of us looking, finding our way again
Out of this mess we're in

She's walking the streets because she has no home
All she has hangs on her flesh and bones
Too many nights sleeping without a warm bed
She passes by but they just turn their heads
Don't know about this mess we're in

Old man dying from too much drink
Blood and glass laying in the bathroom sink
No one stopped to read the words that he wrote
Or care to hear the stories that he told
Don't know about this mess we're in

The smoke is clearing and we see a light
Coming together for a different fight
All of us looking, finding our way again
Out of this mess we're in

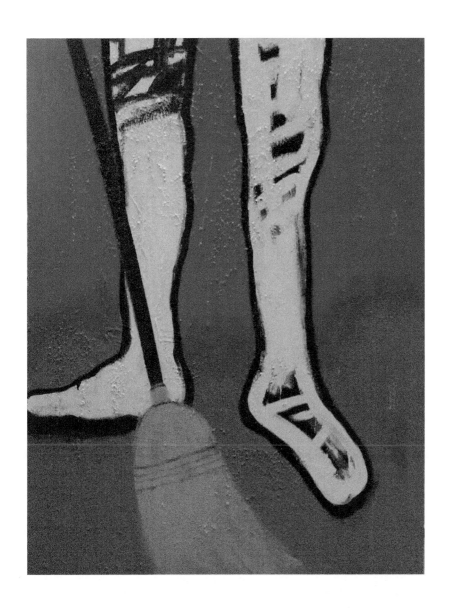

THE BIG RANCH

■ TAKE ME BACK TO *EL RANCHO GRANDE* WHERE THERE IS MUCH JOY

We all looked so happy
When we climbed up on the bus
Berto waved a hand from his seat and said
Good to have you, come ride with us

I got sweet water and a loaf of bread
Should last us about half a day
But you can't have more then a sip of wine
Because we have to stay up most of the way

Laying on a beat old sofa
On the porch when nights were hot
Eating instant mashed potatoes
From a big old iron pot

Never had much to worry about
Slept the night under a bunch of stars
Now all the doors got fifteen locks
And the windows are covered up with bars

Let's go down to the big ranch
The big ranch, the big ranch
Let's go down to the big ranch
The big ranch, the big ranch

Let's go down to the big ranch
The big ranch, the big ranch
Let's go down to the big ranch
The big ranch, the big ranch

Read in the paper just the other day
That the city's now full of guns
Whatever happened to the simple days
When the children could just play and run

I couldn't believe that on New Year's Day
Julia turned around to John and said
This year we're gonna get us a Colt .45
Keep it near us under the bed

Let's go down to the big ranch
The big ranch, the big ranch

Let's go down to the big ranch
The big ranch, the big ranch

Let's go down to the big ranch
The big ranch, the big ranch

LA VENGANZA DE LOS PELADOS

■ THEY'RE COMING TO TAKE YOUR STUFF.

Nosotros somos los de abajo, y eso no se va negar
Como perros en la noche sin una luna a ladrar
Estamos 'bajo de los puentes y abajo de la sombra
Abajo de tus narizes y abajo de la alfombra
Pero les digo, tengan cuidado de la venganza que llegará
La venganza que llegara, la venganza de los pelados
Nos llaman los pelados, y que el Diablo nos llamó
Pero nadie sabe quien, quien era que nos mandó
Ya esconden las memorias y la plata y el pan
Pero para ser seguro nunca poderan
Pero les digo, tengan cuidado de la venganza que llegará
La venganza que llegara, la venganza de los pelados
Pero les digo, tengan cuidado que la venganza ya empiezo
La venganzan de los pelados, la venganza ya comenzó

IS THIS ALL THERE IS?

■ IT'S THE BIG QUESTION, ISN'T IT?

Climbing high to the mountain top
Reaching up to the sky above
Asking myself
Is this all there is?

Sailing into the ocean blue
Trying to find at least one clue
On a paper scrawled
Is this all there is?

And they all came to talk about it
They came to cry and laugh and fight about it
All searching for the promised land
Tired souls with empty hands
Asking themselves
Is this all there is?

Fifteen years on a sewing machine
Where twisted hands don't mean a thing
Wondering to herself
Is this all there is?

Baby crying into an old tin cup
Wanting more but there's never enough
While her mother sighs
Is this all there is?

And they all came to talk about it
The came to cry and laugh and fight about it
All searching for the promised land
Tired souls with empty hands
Asking themselves is this all there is?

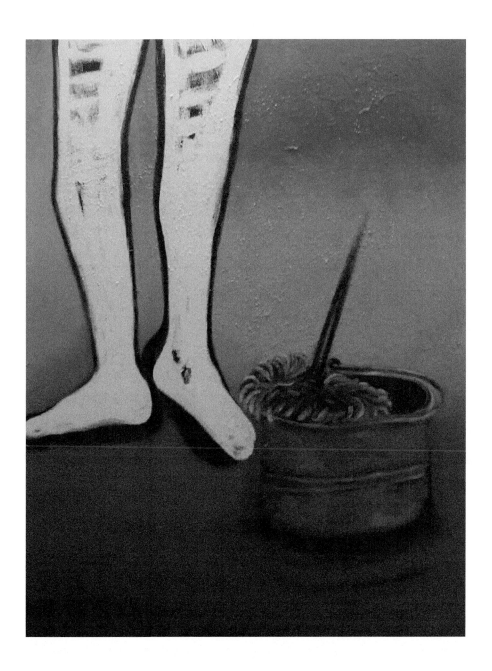

SHORT SIDE OF NOTHING

■ BEING AT THE WRONG PLACE ALL OF THE TIME.

Dreams wash down the gutter
All my hopes in vain
Crows up on the rooftop
Laughing out my name
Here I am on the short side of nothing

We danced all night as life stood by
And we told another lie
Found a spot down by the roadside
There I closed my eyes
And here I am on the short side of nothing

All alone, all alone
Can't find my way home

Summer has come and the heat hangs low
No escape in sight
Sirens scream and lovers moan
Just like any other night
And here I am on the short side of nothing

All alone, all alone
Can't find my way home

seven

DREAMING ABOUT GREEN SHOES,
HAIRCUTS & CAKE

DOSE

■ AIN'T NO DIFFERENCE AMONG US WHEN WE'RE DEAD.

I went to see La Lola just to tell her what I'd done
The things inside my head were far away from gone
"What happens to a kid, Lola, when he grows up brown?"
She said, "Sit down and let me tell you if you wanna stick around"
Poured some coffee in a cup made of Mexican clay
"Sit down right in that chair and listen what I say
Richer men, poorer men, dumber men, sure men
You wouldn't ever think, that they were all made the same"

I laid down on the sofa and fell asleep just yesterday
And in my sleep a guy in white came up to me to say,
"Bet you're wondering why everybody else gets all the breaks
While your mama and your papa and your sister's turning gray"
Made a cup of something hot, some kinda Hindu brew
"Listen to me good 'cause this is all I have for you:
Don't matter who you are, this side or that side of the fence
Or you got a pile of money or you can barely pay the rent
When you die and they take you and they put you in the ground
No matter who or what you are—you end up looking brown"

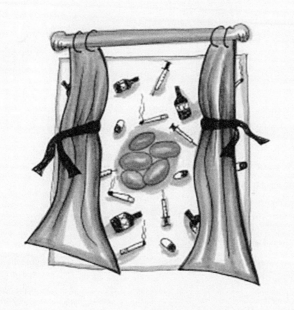

FOREVER NIGHTSHADE MARY

■ SHE NEVER LEARNED TO BE ANYONE ELSE BUT MARY.

Maybe a moonbeam
To light the way when evening comes
Hasn't a worry
Don't care about the cold outside
Only a glad wish
For a magic ride on wings of gold

Only a daydream
Maybe a moonbeam
Just a star bright
Forever nightshade Mary, goodnight

She don't want money
Don't want rings or fancy things
Only a star bright
To shine behind big clouds of joy

Only a daydream
Maybe a moonbeam
Just a star bright
Forever nightshade Mary, goodnight

DREAM IN BLUE

■ IN A BLUE DREAM HE ALMOST DISCOVERED
WHAT WE'VE ALL BEEN LOOKING FOR.

I peeked inside of the open door
Looked around, don't know what for
Way too bright, could hardly see
Oh no, can't believe it
Oh yeah, could almost see it
In a dream in blue

I flew around with shiny things
And when I spoke, I seemed to sing
High above, floating far away
Oh no, can't believe it
Oh yeah, could almost see it
In a dream in blue

Woke up laughing in my bed
A silly smile stuck on my head
Am I real or still in a dream?
Oh no, can't believe it
Oh yeah, could almost see it
In a dream in blue

KIKO AND THE LAVENDER MOON

■ NO ONE KNEW WHAT MY UNCLE FRANK
WAS UP TO WHEN THEY WERE SLEEPING—I DID.

Kiko and the lavender moon
Out playing, makes believe nobody can see
And then he waits
And then he fakes
And then he bends
And then he shakes
He plays and plays
Still playing till he
Goes off to sleep

Kiko and the lavender moon
Out dancing, making faces at a big black cat
And then he flies
Up to the wall
Stands on one foot
Doesn't even fall
Dance and dance
Still dancing till
He goes off to sleep

He always sleeps
Until the sun goes down
He never wakes
Until no one's around
He never stops
Can't catch his breath
It's always there
Scares him to death

Kiko and the lavender moon
Out dreaming about green shoes, haircuts and cake
And then he wishes

The world away
And then he kneels
As if to pray
He dreams and dreams
Kiko and the lavender moon

SAME BROWN EARTH

■ IN THE BEGINNING THERE WAS A LOT OF STUFF GOING ON, OKAY?

The sun came down from black
And from the dim made light
From dumb made a word
In a blink made an eye
And in a beat made a heart
In a beat made a heart

It was when a man was a ribbon set on fire
When man was sea, salt and ash
When woman was a rock on a distant mountain top
When woman was like glass
Reflecting as a mirror

Man was December fog laying low in the valley
And woman was a torch,
Bright in the dark
With full cup and open hand
Gave milk and fed bread to
The lost sons of Adam
Cooking up in kitchens, in rooms
In doom gray tent homes of
The aged or desperate, of the
Drunk and forgotten

So true they rest
Rest in the earth
And become the earth
Under carpets of dandelions
Blowing their seed across the
Breeze, across that same
Brown earth to rise
And sing again
To rise and sing again

LOCOMAN

■ OUR CHICANO SUPERHERO IS A BIT UPSET.

This is all about the Locoman
Who tried to cut the world in two
Wrapped it up in chicken wire
And tried to drag it home to you

The grass and trees and roses
Mixed in with the sand and sea
Laid it out across the table
And got down on his knee

This is all about the time he stumbled
And tore a hole up in the sky
The clouds and thunder rumbled
Like a big truck driving by

This is about the Locoman
Who was all messed up over you
He grew to the size of a mountain
That was all that he could do

JUPITER OR THE MOON

■ IN DESPERATION, SHE ASKS A PLANET AND A MOON FOR ANSWERS.

If I could
Turn night into day
You know I would

If I could
Make stone into gold
You know I would

Looking for why
Up in the sky
Where have you gone
Gone so soon?
Ask Jupiter or the moon

If I could
Move clouds from the blue
You know I would

If I could
Make this day last
You know I would

A quiet sigh
At morning light
Where did you go?
Gone so soon
Wake Jupiter or the moon

Talk to me
Hear me please
How long is forever?
Tell me, Jupiter or the moon

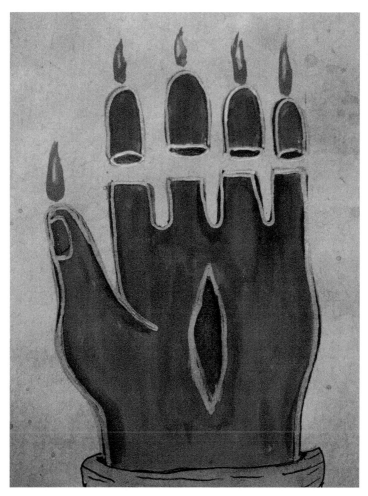

Gazing up
Into the dark
If you could
If you would
You should just
Talk to me
Hear me please
How long is forever?

CHINESE SURPRISE

■ SOMETIMES MYSTERIES ARE REVEALED IN SIMPLE WAYS.

Two skinny dogs yelling at the sky
By a big red tree
Compton neon night
Scrawled on the wall
Almost ten foot tall
In a Chinese surprise in my soup

A boy and a girl hugging on a step
Palm trees sway
To the right and to the left
 Scratched in the tree
"Always" you and me
Like a Chinese surprise in my soup

A little bitty ant crawling in the dirt
The big ole dog
Tugging at my shirt
Let's walk along the road where the wild wishes go
In a Chinese surprise in my soup

COLOSSAL HEAD

■ A PRE-COLUMBIAN OLMEC DANCE GROOVE.

What big eyes you have
What big lips you have
What a nice hat
I love you

What you said?
I can't hear you
What you said?
What you said?

Do the Colossal Head

What you said?
What you said?

What big eyes you have
What big lips you have
What a nice hat
I love you

Do the Colossal Head

CRAYON SUN

■ WHEN YOU'RE FIVE YEARS OLD THAT'S REALLY ALL YOU CAN BE.

Scrunched-up face in a picture booth
Feet don't reach the bathroom floor
Ball goes flying through the air
Neighbors' tree needs me to climb
This is what I am

Crayon sun hung on the fence
Someone laughs at my shoes on wrong
This is what I am

Finger pointed at the moon
A little scared when the thunder rolls
Counting cars from my screen door
Reaching out for a hand to hold
This is what I am

LAGOON

■ MEMORIES OF YOUTH LIKE STILL WATER.

Last night I hung a branch on the wall
To greet the new day, to send me on my way
Footsteps on still water become spirits of gone afternoons
Of Junes by lakes
Evening moons over tired little houses
Of boxcars and fields
Of sloping hills on cardboard slides
Of Sunday drives with windows down
To warm breeze summer nights under backyard stars
Asleep beneath tents of blankets and sticks
Where I play, where I stay
Where a restless dream meets the water
And fades away

Last night I hung a branch on the wall
To meet tomorrow, to send me through my day
Where a gray old dream meets the water
And fades away

MALAQUE

■ SOMEWHERE IN THE JUNGLE A YOUNG BOY
ASKS ABOUT THE MEANING OF LIFE.

Tell me please, dear Malaque
Why have our loved ones gone away
Left with nothing much to say
Only the warm place where they lay
On the way to the Ruby King

Malaque, what do we do
Now that there's only me and you
Can we begin our lives anew
After all that we've been through
On this day of the Ruby King

We have worked so hard to find
What is yours and what is mine
How does one become so blind
And forget what is divine
In the world of the Ruby King
Malaque oh Malaque
Where have our friends all gone today
Gone without a word to say
Only the beds where they once laid
Left to rest with the Ruby King
Gone away to the Ruby King

MANIFOLD DE AMOUR

Voy a navegar
Al puerto del alma
Cruzando el mar
Hasta que llegaré

MUSTARD

So the big ole boy looks like he had enough
Still, he could use a little mustard
Sits and laughs and talks about his groovy life
Can't sleep and steals all the covers

Get back!
When you got it, makes you want some more
Don't want to share a single bit
Come back!
When you ain't got it, makes you want it more
And already it's running out
And already it's running out

When the next-door-Joe goes off into the dark
He's lookin' around for some mustard
And María boils a bone in a big black pot
Tastes like the kind made by her mother

Get back!
When you got it, makes you want some more
Don't want to share even a bit
Come back!
When you ain't got it, makes you want it more
And already it's running out
And already it's running out

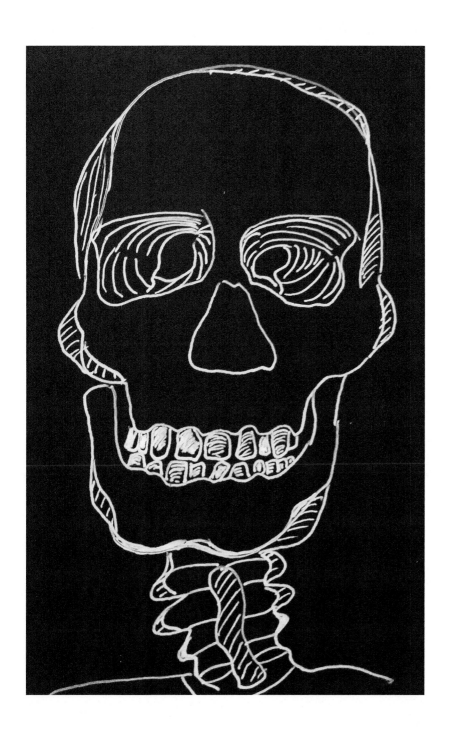

NEW ZANDU

■ SATORI IN EAST L.A.

Zandu cracked the tile
With a pointed file
Could be heard for miles

Diamond cut the glass
Like a blade of grass
Nothing made to last
In the halls of Lu
In the new Zandu

In the halls of Lu
In the new Zandu

In the halls of Lu
In the new Zandu

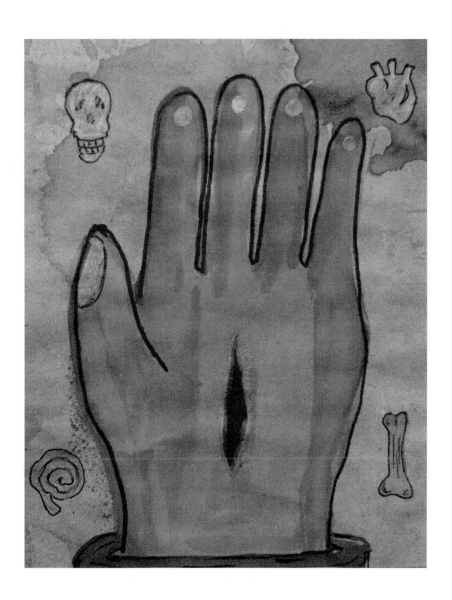

TEN BELIEVERS

■ THEY CAME, THEY SAW, BUT ONLY A FEW OF THEM STAYED.

One light shines in the deep night shining
Two find light in the deep light shining
Three look finding in the bright light shining
Four come looking at the bright light shining
Five go smiling at the light bright shining
Six are lying in the warm light shining
Seven come and seven go
Eight laugh and never know
Nine reap but never sow
Ten believers in a row

TOO SMALL HEART

■ Too Small Heart comes to town
to create havoc for our protagonist.

Too Small Heart got its kicks in Spain
All I found were some shoes in the rain
Too Small Heart split my heart in two
Pieces flying out, way into the blue

Too Small Heart called late last night
Didn't say hello, only goodbye
Said only goodbye
Too Small Heart called me late last night

Ran me down in one, two, three
Like nothing, like saying your ABCs
And when I thought I had enough
Laughed and said, "Boy, it's only love it's just love"
Too Small Heart said, "It's only love it's just love"

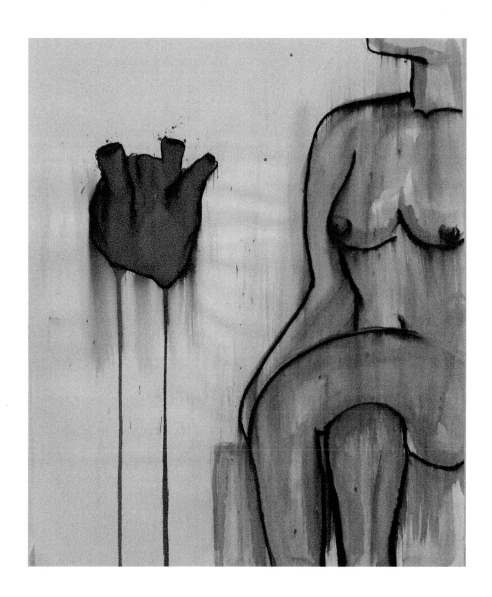

SONG OF THE SUN

■ THE ABORIGINAL CREATION MYTHS SPEAK OF THE WORLD BEING SUNG INTO EXISTENCE. I GUESS FOR THE REST OF US, IT WAS SCREAMED.

In the beginning there was the sun
And it did shine on me
Showed me the way down the road
Along the twists and turns
Through the alleys and through streets
When I couldn't feel the dirt beneath my feet

Then there came the wind
And it did blow dust on me
Made it hard for my eyes to clearly see
Couldn't wash them with my tears
Couldn't see in front of me
Couldn't feel my way through the dark

When fire came to be
And it felt so hot on me
Then burned the flesh of men from their bones
And left their souls to wander
To stagger in a daze
Alongside the bent and broken of the earth

Water was last to come
And it did rain on me
It cooled my broken and bitter heart
It poured down from my face
It ran down to my legs
And soothed me deep into my soul

eight

BIG QUESTIONS

FATHER

■ WHEN YOU THINK ABOUT WHAT IS FATHER, DAD, THE OLD MAN,
I BELIEVE IT IS ALL ABOUT RESTLESSNESS AND SONG.

He never stood still and he tried to look interested and somehow the guise worked
Or was he listening with other parts of the body
Or all of his body, heart, bones, blood
For he did love us
He also did this with all of him
Sometimes for fathers, giving, forgiving, forgetting is done with all these things
"This is for you little *mi hija*, the last piece of cake, the last cup of juice
The last breath I take"
Done responsibly, without remorse, with no resentment
For not tasting chocolate, not quenching thirst, without exhaling

Oh the prayers he said
On that first day of school
On that first sleepover at Rita's
On that first date
Oh the puffs on Camels sitting on the back porch
The late quiet—the reward of being a good man

Flipping morning pancakes so mom could get an extra half-hour
The bubbling coffee
The warm *Chocolate Ybarra*
The *pan de huevo*
"For you first and me last if there is any left, but it's okay and it's all right"
Maybe there is an El Gallo bakery in heaven
And ice cold milk for the Nestle's Quik
Or maybe there is nothing more than the love coming back a million times over

Did I say *gracias*?
Did I say I love you when you checked my covers on a cold night?
Yes I did now and forever

Your songs still play in my brain as if it were springtime in the glow of *ayer*
Sweet mysteries that also live in the outside and inside of me
That is also you, pop, in the everything that I do which is you too
Young man in an old man, old man when you were still young
King of nails, hammers and screwdrivers
Master of hard things and soft things, expert shoelace, prince of pot scrubbing
No one could make toast taste so, so good

LITTLE JOHN OF GOD

■ WHILE IN THE MIDDLE OF A WRITING SESSION MY WIFE MARY PUT A
CARD ON MY DESK FROM THE ST. JOHN OF GOD SCHOOL FOR SPECIAL
CHILDREN AND I WROTE THIS SONG.

He can't run
He can't play
He does things in a different way
Little John, Little John of God

He tries to speak but no one hears
A little boy's pains and a little boy's fears
Little John, Little John of God

He's come to us from up above
To touch our hearts with special love
With special love, Little John of God
You can say with your eyes
What others only say inside
Little John, Little John of God
Little John, Little John of God

BE STILL

■ PEACE, LOVE, AND ALL THAT GOOD STUFF THAT MATTERS.

Let the calm, calm blue waters through
Wash your soul, passing right through you
Like the smallest rose out of the hardest ground
Like a tiny hand reaching up for the sun
Let us hope that our hearts are one
The toughest love is the strongest one
Like a crippled man fights his bitter pain
On two tired legs that hope to walk once again
Just stay gold and be still

As we grow, a river flows
Through our hearts
Finding peace wherever it may go

Let the pure, pure blue waters through
Don't let the wind take them away from you
Like the littlest star that shines in the darkest night
Like a mother's ache that brings in a new life
Just stay gold and be still
Pray that we all can stay gold and be still

TEARS OF GOD

■ FEAR AND PAIN AND FINALLY REDEMPTION.

When it's up to you
To figure out what's right and wrong
It's someone else's parade
And yours is an unhappy song

When it hurts so bad
And you feel that you can't go on
Each day goes by too fast
And the nights are so very long

When your only escape
Is a cheap nickel wine
And the peace you need in your heart
Is so very hard to find

It's a stubborn life we lead
And there's never any rest
Trouble's out there looking for you
Even when you try your best

You'll find out true
What mother said to you
That tears of God will show you the way
The way to turn

Hide not your head
Hear what He once said
He'll show you the way
For there is a world for you and me
Where the blind too can see
Through the tears of God

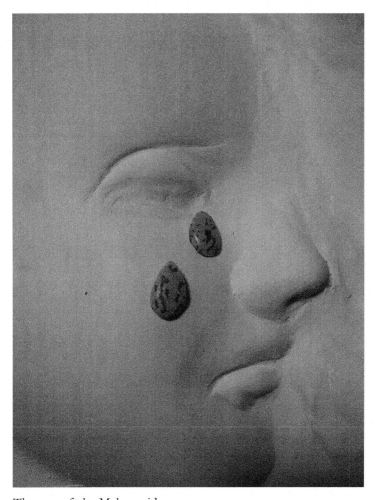

The son of the Maker said
This is my cross to bear
Taking off of our shoulders
Something we should have shared

You'll find out true
What mother said to you
That tears of God will show you the way
The way to turn

SOMEDAY

■ I HAD ALWAYS WANTED TO WRITE
A TRADITIONAL GOSPEL SONG. HERE IT IS.

Someday I will go home
Someday I will go home
And I'll find peace in the house
Of my heavenly father
I will fear, fear no more

I know down in my heart
I know it won't be long
And I shall see the face
Of my savior
I will fear pain no more

Someday I will go home
Someday I will go home
And I shall take the hand
Of my savior
I will feel pain no more
I will feel, I will feel
Pain no more

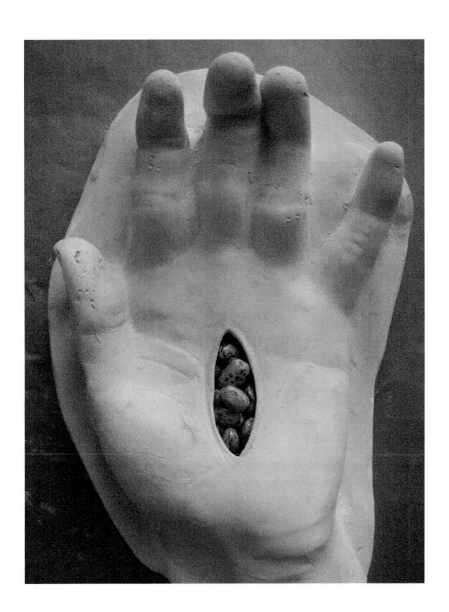

TERESA

■ WRITTEN FOR ST. THERESA OF LISEIUX, THE LITTLE FLOWER

In a motel room on borrowed time
To write the words again
To take them down to pin them on your dress
The church gate opens at ten

On the way I think of wishes
Of all that I could be
But sometimes the things we seem to want
Are not what we really need

Teresa is for the roses
She lets them rain on me
And the one that ies before me
Is the one that sets me free

A rose in the desert sand
Is something that can never be
But a cactus gives a flower
When the thorns are all I see

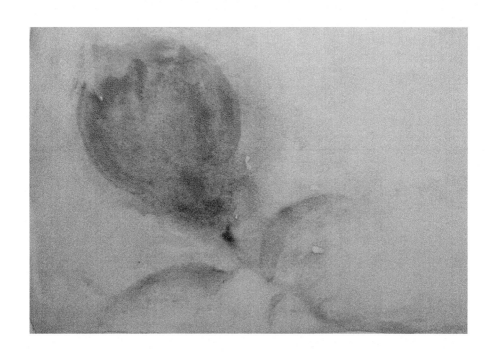

THE LADY AND THE ROSE

■ THE STORY OF AN INDIGENOUS MAN AND AN APPARITION.

On the barren slopes of a thousand hopes
Where a warm wind blows
To a place where I could rest my bones

All my life I've worked the earth
For what it's worth
Sun and dirt is all I've ever known

Gone this way so many times
To make the climb
In the way I always do and will

But this day I heard a sound
As I looked around
And there She was standing on the hill

Blue, the color of her flowing dress
She touched my head with a hand to bless
The color of her skin was brown, like mine
She said in a voice all too divine
"From this day, son, you'll never be alone."
I stood as if my legs had turned to stone

The sweetest music filled the air
Gone were all my cares
Felt like I was walking in a dream

Said, "Pick the roses from around my feet"
They were like something I had never seen
"Take them down to all who don't believe"

MAGDALENA

■ LOOSELY BASED ON THE BIBLICAL FIGURE MARY MAGDALENE.

Magdalena of light and soul
Midnight eyes black like coal

Can I find you among the blessed
And lay my head in your arms to rest?

And keep beside me on this holy road

Magdalena, take my clothes
Give away my jewels and all the gold

Let me walk along the holy road

Magdalena, take my robes
Rid me of this heavy load

Stay beside me on this holy road

IF YOU WERE ONLY HERE TONIGHT

■ SLEEPLESS, STARING DOWN THE CLOCK.

It's 12:02 a.m., another day is gone again
Will the sun be my friend
Or will this night just never end?
Nowhere I could run, at fifteen after one
I wouldn't have did what I had done
If you were only here tonight

What am I to do, when the clock says half past two?
Do I stare out in the dark or try to look for you?
At twenty after three, there's no one up, just me
I wouldn't have did what I had done
If you were only here tonight
It wouldn't have been such a fight
If you were only here tonight

The moon has gone away, lost up in the gray
The birds all in the trees with nothing left to say
Standing at the door, can't believe it's almost four
I wouldn't have did what I had done
If you were only here tonight

I wouldn't have put up such a fight
If you were only here tonight
I wouldn't have did what I had done
Had I known you were here tonight

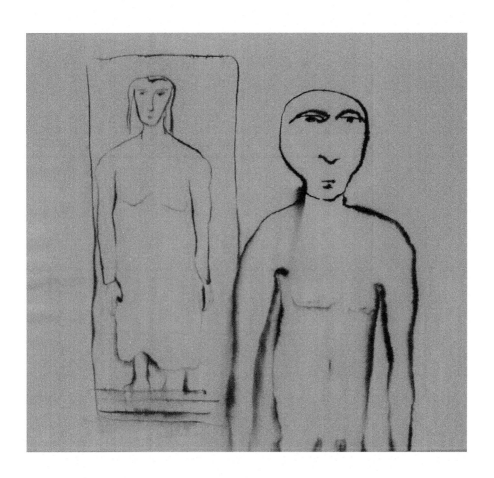

SOMEWHERE IN TIME

■ IN A PLACE FARAWAY

I hear a voice singing somewhere in time
A song I knew so long ago
It takes me back to places somewhere in time
To everyone I used to know

I see a face I remember somewhere in time
Someone I love who's gone away
Gone away somewhere in time
Gone away somewhere in time

Another night, on a highway somewhere in time
Darkness plays those tricks on me
Far down the road in the shadows somewhere in time
Am I the man I'm supposed to be?

I see a light, shining somewhere in time
A lonely light to lead me on
To lead me on somewhere in time
To lead me on somewhere in time

Wake from a dream, a dream from somewhere in time
I rub my eyes so I can see
You're standing there before me somewhere in time
Standing there waiting for me

And I'll take your hand someday somewhere in time
Forever I'll be here with you
I'll be with you somewhere in time
I'll be with you somewhere in time
I'm here with you somewhere in time

HOLD ON

■ STAYING ONE STEP AHEAD OF SELF-DESTRUCTION.

Hold on
Hold on to every breath
And if I make it to the sunrise
Just to do it all over again
Do it all over again
I'm killing myself just to keep alive
Killing myself to survive

Every night I stare this thing down
Knowing that you'll win in the end
There's blood on the rag
And only dust in the bag
Thought you said that you were my friend

Hold on
Hold on to every breath
And if I make it to sunrise
Just to do it all over again
Do it all over again
I'm killing myself just to keep alive
Killing myself to survive

Every day I watch the sun go down
Telling myself a big lie
Can I say I'll go another day
Or will this be the time that I die?

Hold on
Hold on to every breath
And if I make it to sunrise
Just to do it all over again
Do it all over again
I'm killing myself just to keep alive
Killing myself to survive

MANNY'S BONES

■ MANNY GOES HOME—ALL THE WAY HOME.

On the day Manuel went and died
The men all laughed and the girls did cry
Now it's time to lay his soul to rest
Do him up in his Sunday best, oh my

Manny's dead and didn't leave me none
Went off to heaven, left his bed undone
Gone away, he didn't leave a cent
The dogs are all wonderin' where their daddy went, oh my

Don't go leave me here by myself
Won't hear me callin' when you've all done left
Guess I didn't make it out this time
But I'll be waitin' on the other side, bye bye

Way down in Manny's bones
A dry old river and a dusty soul
We'll take him down to the fishin' hole
And let the water take him to his home
Way down in Manny's bones

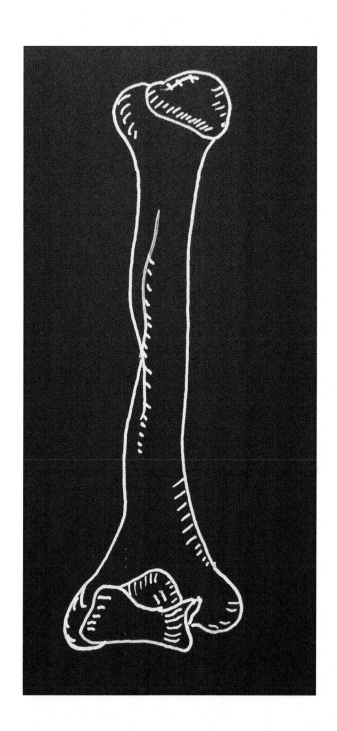

THIS TIME

■ NOT TOMORROW, NOT YESTERDAY, BUT THIS TIME.

Why do the days
Go by so fast?
If only time
Was built to last

If it could learn
To take it slow
Then maybe time
At last would know

That if Monday, Tuesday
Should go away
It'll be Wednesday, Thursday, Friday
Then Saturday
And when Sunday comes
It's just too late
It's gotta be this time

How come the days
Do what they do?
Maybe if time
Time only knew

Could be that time
Don't really know?
That it should try
To take it slow

Then maybe Monday, Tuesday
Won't go away
Then maybe Thursday, Friday
Could be like Saturday
And when Sunday comes

It's never too late
It'll be this time
It's gotta be this time

How come the days
Do what they do?

nine

REFLECTIONS ON MUSIC, ART & LIFE

LOUIE PÉREZ: *UN CHINGÓN* SONGWRITER

■ *by David Alvin*

"So, DO YOU EVER write any serious songs?" The smug Los Angeles radio DJ asked Louie Pérez and David Hidalgo back in 1983.

I was listening at home that evening as Louie and David were being interviewed on a Los Angeles radio station. They were promoting the release of the first Los Lobos LP titled "And A Time To Dance."

Los Lobos had recently signed with L.A.-based Slash Records, the same label that at the time signed my band, The Blasters. Because Slash was legendary for releasing cutting edge albums by local punk rock heroes X and The Germs, maybe the DJ was a little confused as to why Slash had signed "just another band from East L.A." The DJ made reference to all the songs on the DP being lighthearted dance numbers and then snidely asked, "You know what I mean? Do you ever write any hard hitting, heavy songs about serious subjects? Social commentary, that sort of thing?"

"Oh, man," answered Mr. Pérez, "people don't want to hear that sort of stuff from us. We're just a Chicano dance band. We're here to have a good time. We'll leave all the serious social commentary to Dave Alvin and people like that."

I've always remembered Louie's surprising answer on that long ago evening with a smile and not just because he mentioned my name, though that was very kind of him. No, it always makes me smile because on the next Los Lobos album, Louie started writing song lyrics as powerful and "serious" as anything I or any other songwriter at that time, were writing. Suddenly music critics were hailing the arrival of a new master songwriter and the biggest songwriter of the era, Elvis Costello, was singing Louie's sublime and tender lyrics to "A Matter Of Time" in concert. As people sometimes say about painters, athletes, and songwriters, Louie "had the gift."

On that next Lobos album, "Will The Wolf Survive," Louie wrote this line in the title song; "It's truth they all look for, something they must keep alive." This search for truth is the key to survival and that truth is at the heart of so many of Louie's poetic lyrics. It's a heart that eats steadily and relentlessly throughout his work. In deceptively short and simple sentences, Louie hones in on the complex and universal truths of our lives. It's the struggle and suffering we must all endure to survive, driving us to yearn, search, love, pray, to connect with lovers, to God and, perhaps most important for Mr. Pérez, to hope.

From this album onward, nearly every song and nearly every line connects to one or more of these themes in a way that doesn't punch the listener in the face demanding attention or smash them over the head with a "heavy" message. By imbuing the songs of Los Lobos with vivid, unexpected imagery via deceptively simple lyrics, Louie leaves his audience alone to ponder the most visceral experiences of his stories on their own, at any level or point of they choose or perceive.

Louie is a searcher of truth and that quest can't be denied whether you're a philosopher, poet, or a rock and roller. This search for truth creates a force for hope that is the ultimate means for survival. On the 1987 Lobos album, "By The Light Of The Moon," Louie is even more clear that his search for truth is the only way for hope and therefore survival. In the song "Tears Of God," he writes "When it's up to you to figure out what's right and wrong, you'll find out true, what mother said to you, that tears of God will show you the way to turn." By searching for truth, he shows that God sees the struggle of human existence and, for Louie, it's a God of compassion, for God can empathize with us enough that even God cries. With God understanding our pain enough to shed tears, can the mercy of survival be far away? The relief in the hope for God's mercy in the following line is obvious and palpable: "For there is a world for and me, where the blind too can see through the tears of God."

From "By The Light Of The Moon" onwards through "Kiko" and subsequent Los Lobos albums, Louie moved beyond the suffering and goal of mere survival in our lives. Dissatisfied with the chronic struggle, his poetic search for truth goes beyond the earthly plane to what he hopes, he imagines, he believe and yet possibly also doubts to be another better, if intangible, reality. "A boat set into the wind, drifting lost in waters of doubt on a journey that has no end... here on a river of fools." And we are fools, lonely, drifting fools going nowhere and in spite of our ignorance, Pérez finds a "trio of angels holding candles of light to guide the ship to an unknown shore."

Louie the spiritual poet searches for the elusive bridge between life and death. I saw this firsthand when, after decades of talking about trying to find time to write a song together, Louie, David Hidalgo and I finally co-wrote a song. We wrote the lyrics to "Somewhere In Time" shortly after my father had died as well as the tragic death of the wife of Cesar Rosas. Reeling from these losses, we were searching for some truth and consolation, looking for that bridge between the living and the dead.

The lyrics recognized the transitory nature of life in no uncertain terms whether or not we knew it as we wrote them down. Within the three short verses and choruses, the transitional word "somewhere" appears no less than sixteen times, as if it was a soothing mediation or a rosary. Like people holding the "string of beads in a trembling hand heading close to judgment day," that Louie wrote about in "River Of Fools," we were searching for the truth when we wrote the lines in our song of the hope that "forever I'll be here with you… I'll be with you somewhere in time, I'll be with you somewhere in time, I'm here with you somewhere in time."

Often when I'm working on a new song I'm not thinking too deeply about the meaning behind the lyrics. I am mainly concerned that there is some rhythm in the words and that the damn end lines rhyme. Sometimes the meaning of the song is unclear even to me until I've sung it several times or finally recorded it. Sometimes, believe it or not, it can take years of performing a song to at last realize what it's meaning is. But that wasn't the case with "Somewhere In Time." Louie and I knew exactly what we wanted to say and guided each other across that bridge between life and death as we wrote it together. Writing such a transcendental song with Louie was one of my proudest moments as a songwriter.

For the 30 or so years that I've known him, I've been blessed to watch Louie Peréz evolve from a songwriter who imitated the traditional yet inspirational lyrics of American rhythm and blues and Mexican *corridos,* into a darn serious songwriter whose best work stands equal that of those two master songwriters of spiritual exploration, Leonard Cohen and Bob Dylan. Not bad for a guy who claimed he was playing music to make people dance and have a good time.

I think that smug DJ from 30 years ago has finally the answer to his ignorant question. I hope he's listening. I know I am.

David Alvin, *a prolific songwriter, is the co-founder of the musical group The Blasters.*

THE VISUAL ARTWORK OF LOUIE PÉREZ IN 8 TRACKS.

■ *Rodolfo Arana*

ART MUST BE THE RESULT OF A DEEP HONESTY AND WILL BY THE CREATOR.
—DAVID ALFARO SIQUEIROS

Track 1. Connections.

THE FIRST FEW WORDS I exchanged with Louie Pérez were about the subject of San Francisco's Museum of Modern Art (SFMOMA) and a retrospective exhibition of Robert Rauschenberg, which he visited some forty years ago. Louie and I had just met a few years before. I was pleased and a bit surprised he would share with me this artistic reference instead of the traditional hand-shake issued to every fan of the band, Los Lobos. That confirmed for me that Louie's spirit reached even higher than just music.

Some time after our first meeting, I saw a couple of Louie's personal draw-ings. The nature of those drawings drew me closer to the virtual gallery of Louie's alternate band, The Latin Playboys, and along with it a story with a les-son that, curiously, relates more to visual art than music (although I'm a declared fan of Los Lobos). Since that time I have come to know a creator with a par-ticular brand and a creative flow that reaches audiences on different streams.

Using a warm friendly approach, Louie shares with us part of his work, from the simplest graphite drafts drawn on the road during his concert tours going back more than forty years ago, to the more precise and elegant works such as the ones in the "Dream of Beans" series. His visual art reveals clear evidence of his own Mexican roots, but also the universality of an artist capable of clustering many stories into a few strokes.

This creator's career is definitely linked to his own personal life, family roots, the languages he was exposed to as a child: English as a native tongue in his birthplace and Spanish which permeated among his relatives who arrived from a different land with their music and words. In addition, the Barrio Latino heritage and personal identity within the US as well as the social changes Louie experienced growing up. All of this sparked in him a singular understanding of his place in the worlds of art and music.

Mexico as "seen" from the other side of the border, for someone who has Mexican blood, is rarely ever the same as the one experienced by those of us who live in *méjico*. That Mexico is more of an evocation than a tangible reality; it feels more like the postcards from far off relatives, like old family pictures, like the tales of ancient gods and celebrations. Mexico is a place where the memory recreates what it has. There is a special place for symbols as powerful as death itself, a character depicted in our art over and over with a thousand faces, from the mythical trip to Aztlán to the trail that leads to the last fringes of Mictlán: the Mexica Underworld. There is something in Mexican art capable of turning death and the act of dying into a work of art present in the iconography of many different ethnic groups who amaze us with their sculpted skulls, tombstones, and funerary monuments crafted as a symbol of space, time, and the creation of humankind itself.

Louie has also recreated Mexico through his own family and an even greater family, namely the artists. He has contemplated *La muerte pintada* by José Guadalupe Posada and the iconic works of Diego Rivera, Gerardo Murillo "Dr. Atl," José Clemente Orozco, Frida Kahlo, and María Izquierdo. But he has also seen Mexico through the eyes of foreign artists such as Jean Charlot, Henry Moore, Antonin Artaud, Max Ernst, Remedios Varo, Leonora Carrington, and André Breton, who meditated and shared their vision about this place that for the ancients was the navel of the world. The ancestral blood seeps into the veins of those who contemplate these works, and that is exactly what I believe happened to Louie Pérez.

TRACK 2. Walking along Whittier Boulevard.

It's clear to me that Louie Pérez has developed two stories around music and culture: his musical journey with Los Lobos (which can be hardly summarized in a few lines) and his personal history of musical encounters, much more intimate and invaluable. The latter is the part that is demonstrably tied to this contemplation of literature, drawing, and the arts—he recalls fondly the first concert he attended, when he was a teenager, of the inimitable Jimi Hendrix. While in high school he met face-to-face with rock & roll through the interpretations of Chicano bands such as Little Willie G and Thee Midniters in the heart of East L.A. When he heard Mexican music played by his neighbors, he knew his familiar roots were tied to those songs.

This part of his musical journey is what enriched the soul and heart of Louie Pérez and subtly influenced his visual, plastic works. From here arose countless experiences that have been transformed into graphic stories rich with symbolism. Much of the music he created has also been drawn, and from it has been visualized through forms that have since become songs. The music and the songs have always been intertwined. It's a seamless loop of creativity—music become visual art and the visual expression contributing to lyrics and melodies. I am not surprised that this artist draws his compositions while he is writing them as a fundamental part of his creative process.

In the 1970s and 1980s Louie Pérez was influenced by a powerful and vibrant L.A. Chicano plastic movement, mingling amongst young personalities like Los Four—Carlos Almaráz, Judithe Hernández, Frank Romero, Beto de la Rocha, and Gilbert Luján. (Judithe Hernández always had a whimsical time explaining how she was the fifth member of a "group of four.") Louie also rubbed creative elbows with talented painters Richard Duardo, John Valadéz, Chaz Bojorquez, and others. Within this environment Louie absorbed experiences that allowed him to develop his plastic process, and to gain knowledge and appropriation of the language that has given him the identity he represents in the visual field.

This Chicano community in Los Angeles and throughout the American Southwest transformed over the years into the generation of Latino artists who are now part of the intellectual art world, featuring their works in galleries and museums, and where Pérez fits legitimately in this unique and powerful realm of the arts.

TRACK 3. An inheritance of Jack Kerouac.

To consider the fundamental work of Louie Pérez, the "creator-maker," is to plunge into a plastic journey that spans more than four decades and begins precisely in the legendary community of East Los Angeles, where social movements in the world of the 1960s and 1970s were inspired. That time and place was the catalyst for a great diversity of forms, structures, and trends in the arts and culture (painting, music, literature.) It was a dynamic time. It was, among other things, the time of metamorphosis of the Age of Aquarius and the screams of Ginsberg, Kerouac, or Burroughs, along with the magic of Jimi Hendrix, Miles Davis, Bob Dylan, and The Grateful Dead that vibrated at that time, all merging with arts movements.

I recognize the literary equivalent of painting's "gesturalism" in works such as "On the Road" or "Orizaba 210 Blues" or "Los Subterráneos" in much of the discourse that Pérez has managed to evoke in his stories, tales, and plastic works, with all the contemplation of our time, of our lives, but also making a triumphant metamorphosis of this inheritance throughout his work.

TRACK 4. The symbolic encounter with 'el Maestro de Maestros.'

Louie Pérez has repeatedly mentioned his great appreciation for Davíd Alfaro Siqueiros as one of art's most iconic figures. He particularly appreciates Siqueiros' masterful El Coronlelazo (The Great Colonel). I dare to say it is his most important work, La Marcha de la Humanidad, that has given an appropriate and personal meaning to Louie's art, both for its social reference (the "masses" before the world), and for the plasticity, majesty, and relentless strength in its forms, its colors, its expressions. It was inevitable for Louie Perez to have discovered in 1971 the book "Siqueiros" written by Mario de Micheli, which transformed his perception of art and ultimately focused it in the plastic arts.

Art itself brings with it a creative freedom. In Louie's works it becomes relevant for its creative force, accentuating his appreciation of and gratitude for Siqueiros, before his personal metamorphosis by the plastic arts.

TRACK 5. Reflections regarding Mexican art.

Pérez's artistic iconography definitely focuses on the concept of "Being," and its manifestation in the world around him. In his paintings and drawings the symbolism of all their roots is revealed. It brings about a new meaning that enhances them within a unique visual language: the Santitos, the Guadalupana, and the mystical life, the bean as a reflection of the identity of the original Mexico (an example of this is the graphic series "Dreams of Beans"), or the actual calaca as a character that moves among us every day. These images offer the creator a wide opening to an iconic, diverse visual world. Louie Pérez's work feeds on this aspirational contemplation of the visual mysticism of the Mexican roots, nourishing its iconography in his plastic work.

TRACK 6. Death seen from the mirror of art.

It's interesting how Louie deals with "death" as reflected in his plastic works. Some of his works filter the inheritance of personalities such as José Guadalupe Posada. Such works adopt his forms and gestures, molding paintings with firm and wide strokes. This is complemented with subtle qualities of softness and charm. It is similar in its visual applications to the characters painted by Chucho Reyes, but also reflected by countless artisans, labels, bakers, and street artists, mostly anonymous, who have reflected the death image in public display cases, breads, rice paper, or walls, turning it into a universal character, contemplated with serenity and confidence. It's hard to achieve this without breaking the reliability and dexterity of a work of art. Pérez achieves it flawlessly. Death in art, forever alive.

TRACK 7. Opening the door to the contemporary world.

I am convinced that despite adopting a profound influence from Mexican culture and art (notably Siqueiros but also Rufino Tamayo, Diego Rivera, Jose Guadalupe Posada, or María Izquierdo), Louie's work reveals other important influences. Parallel to the Chicano plastic movement of his upbringing, Louie Pérez "the plastic maker" has been able to discover for more than four decades in art references as diverse, relevant, and universal as Marcel Duchamp, Joseph Beuys, Georg Baselitz, Henry Moore, Robert Rauschenberg, Philip Guston, Betye Saar, Nancy Spero, Diane Arbus, and Kiki Smith. This mixture has given him the flexibility to fuse plastic languages that he has managed to achieve his own unquestionable language, making him a conceptual maker of forms in this contemporary world.

TRACK 8. Work materials, much like fingerprints.

Although much of Louie Pérez's work is based on oil techniques (portraits, mainly), and has even developed pieces in sculpture, the Californian is an accomplished draftsman who has reflected the daily transit of life in his works. His graphic stories, full of nostalgia and harmony, awaken a variety of emotions. He conjures themes that are appropriate with his particular style of "traditional" techniques of drawing such as inks, watercolors, mixed media, and acrylic, opening the doors of his making in the process of creation itself.

CONCLUSION. Louie the inspirer.

More than four decades later, that boy from East L.A., with a Mexican heritage that caught dreams to turn them into stories, letters, and paintings, has today become a creator of American cultural history. I would say Louie Pérez represents a new "classic" of the art world. He is an inspirer of the new generations that have grown along with him through his works and who has worldwide recognition for all he has managed to create—in art, in music, and in life itself.

Rodolfo Arana *is a visual artist and art critic. He lives in Mexico.*

Translation from Spanish by Jorge García Aguilar.

AN INTERVIEW WITH LOUIE PÉREZ

■ *by David Greenberger*

Louie Pérez and David Greenberger have known each other for a couple of decades. What started out as mutual interest in and respect for each other's work grew into a lifelong friendship, as they both have continued their creative pursuits while growing older as artists, husbands, and fathers.

DAVID GREENBERGER: Let's talk about the experience of working in different creative realms. You write poems and songs and compose music. You also do work as a visual artist—drawing and painting. Do they play off each other with their commonalities or do they exist separate from each other?

LOUIE PEREZ: The visual art, the music, the words—they all seem to come from the same place. Although it's probably a subconscious process, working in different mediums is an experience in which all the work is related and everything sort of dovetails with everything else. I suppose it began with making pictures—the visual. When I was a little kid I was interested in drawing pictures, captivated by the imagery around me. I focused on the obviously beautiful and on what seemed ordinary. I looked at the lines on the cracked ceiling in my house and I looked at the patterns of the peeling wallpaper. I was fascinated by those shapes and patterns, like a lot of kids are. I started to have fun drawing, making pictures. That interest in the visual has always stayed with me. As I grew older I learned more about how to make art.

GREENBERGER: Did that happen by learning some of the formal rules about art?

PEREZ: After graduating from high school, I went to East Los Angeles College. I was into music so I decided to take music classes—theory and harmony. But I was already a musician at the time and so I got a bit bored with these classes. I started taking art classes instead. I was befriended by a couple of good teachers there who saw potential and encouraged me. I learned much from them. They helped me out a great deal and I owe them a lot. In those classes I studied rock bottom fundamentals, about using various materials and techniques. And I experimented. I developed a kind of intuition about my artistic aesthetic—and of course that there's probably nothing more subjective than art.

GREENBERGER: The subjective and the objective are constantly crashing into each other. I guess you just need to keep yourself from looking at the crash site too closely!

PEREZ: What I say about the songwriting partnership between David Hidalgo and me is this: David is a musician who thinks like a painter and I'm a painter who thinks he's a musician. [LAUGHS]

As time went by, music became more important in my life. But the art stayed with me. I didn't consciously relate drawing pictures to writing songs. I later realized that when I thought about lyrics, I visualized the people, places, and things I was writing about. For example, if there was any "action" happening in the song or if there was any activity depicted—human movement—it's from imagining "seeing" a person as if he or she were walking through the door. I don't think that's too unusual. Writers need to believe their characters are real people. It connects the visual to the task of writing and, in my case, writing songs. It becomes a kind of cinematic process. Visualizing what is happening and, as a result, making a personal connection.

GREENBERGER: As artists, we all need to find a way to connect ourselves honestly with whatever it is we're doing—to get at some essential truth, something we believe and then hope others will believe as well.

PEREZ: Correct. I think we were all born with this need to express ourselves. As little kids in elementary school we made crayon drawings in class that we brought home to show our moms. Our first gallery show was on the refrigerator door. [LAUGHS]

GREENBERGER: And we hopefully learn that maybe everything we make doesn't get kept forever. Or that it can end up with coffee stains and fingerprints on it!

PEREZ: Maybe some drawings will stay on the refrigerator door for a while.

GREENBERGER: Are you writing songs constantly, or do you wait until there's a specific album that has to be recorded then write songs for that project?

PEREZ: I'd like to say I'm writing songs all the time, but I'm not. I don't sit in a hotel room after a gig and write songs. Part of this is the logistics when you tour as a band; the other part is being exhausted after a show. It seems like we're constantly on the road these days.

The only days we have off are those that show up because we can't get to the next town in time to play. There are distractions and sometimes not a lot of "free time" for things such as writing. When I finally sit down to work, it feels like I'm re-inventing the wheel. As if I've never done this before. There's a process of getting myself into the frame of mind to start working. I have to crack it open and get inside this thing, whatever it is. Once I get inside, I'm relieved. It doesn't feel like I'm just breaking rocks—like a prisoner on a road gang doing hard meaningless work.

Every time I go to work on something new, I feel I'm chipping away at this piece of stone, waiting for something to reveal itself. Usually when I haven't worked for a while. Once I'm in the mode, I'm good; the process of writing a song gets underway. I begin to see and hear things differently. I'm in tune with the sensations, observations, and visual things that help in constructing a song.

GREENBERGER: Do you consider the shape of your life, the longevity of it, or the realization there's a diminishing amount of time in front of you? Does that affect your urge to create, in whatever media it may be?

PEREZ: Yes. The fact is I'm getting older. Actually, I don't know anyone who is getting any younger. I'm now in my sixties and I do think about the time I have left. Not to sound morbid but there are certainly more Christmases behind me than there are in front of me. I'm struggling to find the redeeming part of getting old. There's supposed to be wisdom showing up but I'm still waiting. Seriously, I do believe what we have is this accumulated knowledge. We've acquired this from a great deal experience. Whether we want to call it wisdom or knowledge, it doesn't matter. What's important is that it's solid usable stuff whether we're artists, writers, or bricklayers. For inspiration, I often find myself going back to my childhood in East Los Angeles. There's a great wealth of experience there. It makes its way into everything I write about, everything I make whether those experiences are good or bad or indifferent.

GREENBERGER: Yes, as we get older our vantage point on our past changes. It's perhaps less accurate as a documentary of our life, but more resonant poetically. In fact, when we're young we don't have the layers of analysis and introspection that we bring to our observations once we've matured. But there can also be a beautiful "unfilteredness" to whatever memories we reach back and grab.

PEREZ: Absolutely. I grew up on Hammel Street in East Los Angeles. My father had a lot of skills and did what ever it took to support us. Unfortunately, he died young, at forty-six, when was I eight years old. It's a chapter in my life without any words. My mother crossed the border into El Paso from Mexico with my grandmother. She found herself working alongside her mom as a cook on cattle ranches in Laramie and Cheyenne, Wyoming. She came to Los Angeles in the 1920s and worked as a sewing machine operator. It was in Los Angeles where she met the man who became my father.

GREENBERGER: You put it perfectly when you called it "a chapter in my life with no words." I know what you mean. Whatever we're experiencing is just our reality and we usually have no basis of comparison. We may look back on something years later and assign it a label of sadness. Yet, we may well have been perfectly happy at the time.

PEREZ: My childhood was, by and large, a happy one. We didn't have much, but I didn't know what poor was. I didn't know what rich was either. What I watched on television was so different from my own reality. This didn't mean much to me as a kid. I enjoyed playing alone, building things out of sticks and rocks I found in the yard. I guess you can call those structures my first "site specific" sculptural pieces. [LAUGHS] Yeah, it was fun—I had to make up things on my own. I didn't have a father to do the typical father and son stuff, so I became more cerebral. Not that I was smarter or any better than the kid that plays ball in the street. I guess the inside of my head was my playground. My mother was a good mom; she did the best she could do with limited resources. When I look back, I'm actually amazed at what she did, like a lot of moms did in East L.A.

GREENBERGER: Did your mother speak Spanish to you at home?

PEREZ: My mother didn't speak much Spanish at home. She was raised for the most part in the United States. But she was very Mexican in every thread and fabric of her being. At the same time, she was proud to call the United States her home, just like my dad did when he was alive. She loved *ranchera* music. Her favorites were Miguel Aceves Mejía, Lola Beltran, and Antonio Aguilar. She'd listen to Spanish-language radio all day long, although she'd rarely spoke Spanish to my sister and me. I learned to speak it from my grandmother who lived in a little house my dad built for her in our back yard.

My mother didn't speak much about her own personal history, like many immigrants. I'm sure it was a painful experience for her. For immigrants, this process of making the transition, coming from their homeland to another place and, in a sense, losing who they are is something they'd like to forget.

The changes are dramatic. The experiences they had in the 1920s and 1930s, and even till this day, coming to the US wasn't exactly a trip to Disneyland. There were challenges and a great deal of struggle. My mother was reluctant to talk about her story.

GREENBERGER: Her desire to assimilate meant you were being raised as a sort of typical American boy.

PEREZ: Yes, very much so. I watched American sitcoms and cartoons on television, read comic books. The cartoon character Popeye was the first thing I ever drew. As far as music was concerned, Mexican music was constantly playing in the house on the radio as well as records my mother played. When I got tall enough to reach the dial on the brown Bakelite radio, I discovered choice— I could change the dial. That's when I found rock & roll. I have to thank my mom. She loved music and it was always in the house.

Mom would take us downtown to the Million Dollar Theater to see the *variedades,* Mexican variety shows, with singers and vaudeville type acts. After the shows she would drag us backstage and get autographs from the headliners and other performers. Later on, when I showed an interest in music, she encouraged it. She bought me my first guitar when I was maybe around 12 years old. She saved up her *centavos* and bought a guitar from Milan's Music Store on First Street in East Los Angeles. She brought it home and presented it to me— I was off and running.

GREENBERGER: Then somewhere along the line you realized you too could create songs of your own, that your life experiences and observations could be the starting point, or fuel, for the process. In many of your songs there is something I would call a "plausible fiction." I think a believability quality can emerge in a song that needn't even have narrative components—still there is an emotional believability. There's also another aspect you draw upon where there is a character's voice that gives the listener the glimpse of someone whom they can believe over the course of the several minutes of the song.

PEREZ: Yes, that is really interesting. When I begin to work on a song it is not like I have the entire thing completely fleshed out. It's a mysterious process I have to trust. I have to focus on trying to make things work as they reveal themselves. The ideas for songs sometimes come from a line or a phrase I might have heard in a conversation—this can get the wheels turning.

For example, I was listening to the basic track of a song we were recording in the studio. It had this kind of rural sound to it with mandolins and acoustic guitars playing in the background. It gave me the image of traveling through new territory, a new place, like what my mother went through. I imagined the experience she had coming from Mexico, crossing the border to the United States, and this phrase popped into my head: Gates of Gold. I asked myself, "What could be beyond those Gates of Gold?" We might have heard something about what it would be like on the other side. In reality it is the unknown that we are traveling to. It could be a migrant worker or a person coming to the United States. It could also be the question: "What will we find after this life is over?" At that point, all I had was a title and a few images in my head. But it was that title I built this entire song around. Those are the times you get lucky and it keeps you coming back for more.

GREENBERGER: Yes, it's a process that can take various forms and lead to many possible directions.

PEREZ: That's right. A similar thing went on with the writing of the song "Good Morning, Aztlán," which Los Lobos did several years ago. Again, the song started with a phrase that eventually became the title. The idea was to depict what goes on during a typical morning in East L.A., the mundane everyday activities as the world is waking up.

The lyrics describe the pile of dishes in the sink that have to be washed; how the dad in the story is hurrying out of the door to get the kids to school before he's late to work. The narrator is listing in verses all the things that make up a day. Then he breaks in to remind you he's telling the story, and adds, "I gotta say one, two, three more things before I go on." I was looking for something to tie the verses together so I got the idea of having the narrator introduce himself. Once again I got lucky it worked melodically and lyrically as well.

GREENBERGER: I love that line. It makes me really like the narrator. It makes him real. I also like how the dishes are stacked "from the ceiling to the floor," which is the opposite way it's normally described based on our gravity-based thinking. Visually, the stack can be looked at from bottom to top or top to bottom.

PEREZ: Plus I somehow got it all to rhyme!

GREENBERGER: Very important!

PEREZ: I also have to consider that David Hidalgo, my collaborator, is going to be singing the words. I have to write something I believe he would say, so I anticipate that. I've done this with him so many times over the years that now it's become intuitive. We trust each other in the process and that trust is what really makes it work.

GREENBERGER: The album "Kiko" marked a turning point for Los Lobos, both in terms of musical innovation and in lyrics that embraced a greater fluidity. There was less specificity, more mysteriousness and poetics.

PEREZ: I believe the key to the writing for that record was the sense of freedom I felt going in. In 1987 Los Lobos had a worldwide hit with a cover of Ritchie Valens' "La Bamba" from the movie of the same name. The band toured the world, enjoyed all the perks that came with having a number one record, but at the end of that long day it left us wondering what to do next. We decided to challenge all expectations and released the unlikely follow-up, "La Pistola y el Corazón," a collection of traditional Mexican songs, which most music critics considered commercial suicide. What followed that album was a rock record called "The Neighborhood." It was as if we were checking our inventory as well as going back through our history.

We had returned to our rock roots and to our beginnings as a folkloric group. As a songwriter I felt I had cleaned the slate—it was extremely liberating. It was 1992 and I began writing for a new record, the record that became "Kiko." What was different was I didn't feel like I had to adhere to any formula. I had cleared the way for pure uncompromised expression. The songs just flowed as if they had lives of their own.

GREENBERGER: Also you needed to keep yourself true to some foundational ideas otherwise you are floating in a million directions. You've to be heading towards something, even if you don't know exactly what that something is.

PEREZ: This is true. That's where the economy of the things I write comes into play. I need to tell a story from beginning to end in three and a half minutes. I have the visual in my head. I have the story. I don't really feel I need to describe it all. I don't feel it's necessary for me to fill in all the blanks even though it leaves its subject to interpretation. I welcome that—if someone can interpret the song into their own lives by the vehicle of emotion, I think I've succeeded.

GREENBERGER: Ultimately the audience is a part of the process. Your finished work finds a new level of completion in each person who connects with it, each one slightly different than the other.

PEREZ: That's right. I'm not that concerned whether it's the same idea I started with as long as it resonates with the listener. I believe you can capture the essence of something with just a few lines without having to hit them over the head with what you intended. It applies to songs and to visual art. It's kind of a Zen-like process that uses a few simple strokes to convey a thought or sentiment. When the audience engages, it's as if they are reliving the creation of the song or art.

GREENBERGER: How much Mexican culture, history, and tradition find a way into your work?

PEREZ: It's where it starts. My ancestral roots are in Mexico with its incredible richness in history and tradition. But I was born and raised in the United States and shaped by the contemporary realities of the US. I can say that, as Chicanos, we are Mexican-American in its purest definition because we can proudly draw from both. In my work I inevitably refer to both cultural sources. Those ideas and traditions naturally make their way into my work.

GREENBERGER: Do elements of cultural and historical tradition always positively infuse your work, or can they sometimes be a kind of limiting obstacle to overcome?

PEREZ: No, because what I do is tradition in a genuine sense. Tradition moves forward and another generation picks it up and takes what they need from it. They maintain its integrity, but they also have their own interpretation. Keep in mind we started Los Lobos to play Mexican folkloric music in the early 1970s as teenagers, which was unheard of then. We were rock & roll kids growing up with Mexican music playing in the background. We heard this kind of music on Spanish-language radio and from records that our parents played. We never gave it much attention until one day we decided it would be cool to learn an old traditional tune and play it for one of our mother's birthdays. We were absolutely knocked out by how complex and challenging it was to our musicianship. It was like we discovered something that we just about tripped over everyday. It was so exciting and interesting we dedicated ourselves to it for ten years. We surprised a lot of people in those early years of playing traditional Mexican music because we looked like most young people of our generation with long hair, beat up jeans, and flannel shirts.

Some people were downright shocked when we began to play. Young or old, they were all confused with what we were doing. The point is we were playing this music, but doing it in our own way. We respected the music but we also infused it with the energy that we knew from rock & roll. It was a great and fun time for us as a band.

Eventually, we made the full circle back to rock & roll. We found ourselves in this position where we had accumulated a lot of musical history along with the collective experience we had growing up in East Los Angeles. We temporarily put down the Mexican folkloric instruments and picked up the electric guitars again. We made the trip across the L.A. River and into the Hollywood clubs where a lot of exciting musical ideas were going on. Thanks to bands like The Blasters and X we were welcomed into that community. During the time we were playing that scene, we came to the attention of music journalists and record labels. That led to our first recording for a major record label. Then, of course, we hit the road.

There we were, four Mexican American kids from East L.A. "going out to find America." In the process we discovered that instead of finding differences, we found similarities. This struck a nerve. I realized we are all in this thing together—that we have much in common no matter where we come from or how we were raised, whether it be in this country or the rest of the world. I had the opportunity to get up close and personal with the people, places, and things I had only heard about. I was determined to write about this.

GREENBERGER: It is not political in the way that it's framed, but if somebody finds an emotional way into it, you are suddenly building a bridge between two seemingly different things through a kind of gentle side door that nobody knew was there. You came in sort of poetically rather than banging on the front door and handing out leaflets.

PEREZ: That's exactly right. We traveled throughout the United States at a time when—it's hard to believe now—there weren't a lot of Mexican people. Places like Burlington, Vermont or in the South like Chapel Hill, North Carolina. Somewhat, strangely, with our presence we were sort of demystifying and redefining "the Mexican" to a lot of people throughout the country. We realized we were part of something important; there was a subtext to what we were doing. Every night we just went up on stage and played what we always played and we weren't embarrassed by it. We didn't censor ourselves. I think people understood we were sincere and we really meant it.

GREENBERGER: Traveling can be learning, about the world and about yourselves.

PEREZ: Yeah, we traveled way down into the Deep South. As cliché as it may sound it was clear music is the universal language. We toured through places where there was not a Mexican face anywhere. The audiences responded purely because they were moved by the music. People were having a genuine great time. Looking back, it was an incredibly valuable experience for us to get out there and really see the rest of the world. After that first tour we eventually, over the years, toured around the world. I remember some years back, sitting on a pair of patio chairs at a hotel in Perth, Australia, with my band mate David, looking out at this panoramic view of the Indian Ocean. There we were, ten thousand miles from home, two kids from East L.A., staring in awe. That's when David leaned over and said, " Wow, who would've ever imagined we'd be sitting here, who would have thunk it?" Then we busted out laughing.

After all these years, we just keep on doing it. We make music—we make art—simply because that's what we do. We don't really think about it. We just do it.

David Greenberger *is an artist working multiple creative disciplines, best known for his long-running publication* The Duplex Planet. *Through the 1980s he was bass player and songwriter in the band Men & Volts.*

LOS LOBOS: FROM RADIO TO EXPERIENCE

■ *by Martha González*

Los Lobos on the Radio

THE FIRST TIME I heard "La Bamba" performed by Los Lobos it brought tears to my eyes. Like most mornings, I was riding the bus from the Boyle Heights neighborhood of East L.A. to Bancroft Jr. High School in Hollywood, California. I was 13 years old. It was 6:45 a.m. and "La Bamba" was blasting on KROQ FM. This was unusual because KROQ FM was, in my eyes, a very "white" radio station. It wasn't like KDAY FM, which played music by African American artists to the beat of soul, Hip-Hop, and R&B. On this morning ride KROQ was playing something in Spanish! At that moment I didn't know who the artist was; all I knew was that these guys were rocking out a Mexican traditional tune.

It was the classic switch in musical approach at the very end that did it for me. That is to say the shift the Lobos make from a rock rendition to the traditional sound of "La Bamba" which it is well known for. The *jaranas* and the *requintos* took over for the electric guitars for that coda. This traditional shift was a moment of great pride for me. So much so that my heart swelled to a breaking point as tears rolled down my face. The disc jockey then went on to say, "That was Los Lobos from East L.A." and I was floored! Wow! They were from my neighborhood and from where this big yellow bus had just picked me up! This was us on the radio and I was filled with gratitude, felt utterly inspired, and proud to be me.

Los Lobos as Musicians

Some years later I met Los Angeles musician Quetzal Flores and became the singer for the band Quetzal, which he had founded. Flores was a staunch Los Lobos fan and turned me on to all of the Lobos' repertoire. I was instantly enamored with the music. One particular listening session we were working

252

an early Quetzal tune called *"Pasa Montañas"* and he played "Be Still" for me, which is on the "In the Neighborhood" album that was released in 1990. I remember it distinctly because it had a very strong sense of tradition but with a very different sound inflection.

Most memorable for me was the *Huasteco* line. Over the years I have listened to many East L.A. bands from various generations. Like no other band from East L.A., Lobos' compositions create a voyage into other arenas of your psyche. It is quite simply a sonic representation of what it means to be Chicano in East L.A., both lyrically and sonically. The music is, of course, always top-notch but the kind of vision, *sentimiento*, and Chicano angst that it invokes well; I attribute this to Louie Pérez's lyrical prose. Louie is the master of giving you the not-so-typical thought in a very ordinary way. I don't mean this to sound simplistic. I mean it in the best sense of the word, that the most beautiful things are said quite simply. The phrases, ideas and or pictures Louie paints for us take a minute before they hit you. But when they do, it is life altering. The images in "When the Circus Comes to Town" and "Angels with Dirty Faces" provide examples of that. The linguistic schizophrenic *"Más y Más"* provides another illustration of that. "These lyrics, like so many others in the Lobos repertoire, draft a universe for the listener. It is a universe that delves deep into an intimate consciousness. It is quite simply a ride through our heads. Like no other songwriter, Louie has the ability to show our cultural and social complexities. Our losses, our *orgullos*, our triumphs, in our own language no less. Spanish, English, Spanglish it's all utilized. To show this kind of thought process and complexity of a Chicano consciousness is important on many levels.

So often as people of color we are reduced to simpleton antics. Media stereotypes have falsely constructed one-liner ideas of who we are as Mexicans and Chicanos. We are reduced to chimichangas and Speedy Gonzalez, and these kinds of representations have a direct bearing on how our histories and legacies are narrated. When really as Chicanos, our histories, music, art, poetry, dress, language, culture, semiotics, are complex. Our expressions also vary in style. You can find the range of emotions and Chicano worldviews in Los Lobos' sonic and lyrical representations and particularly in Louie Pérez's lyrics.

Los Lobos as Familia

The generosity and general life lessons of love and camaraderie are not just lyrical but rather extend into how Los Lobos works as a band. The memory of struggle and life in the barrio are present in their psyche. I know this first hand as I have been on the receiving end of this sister/brotherhood. In 2003 our band Quetzal was fortunate enough to go on several tour runs with Los Lobos across the United States. This was an amazing opportunity for our band at an early moment in our career. We had been on some small tours but really needed the big road experience. Furthermore, our record company Vanguard was willing to provide some tour support, which alleviated expenditures a bit. So, it was 2003 and we were on the road with Los Lobos!

In the course of the various runs opening for Los Lobos, we were exposed to new cities, musical frontiers, and the Lobos' extensive repertoire as their set lists varied from night to night. It was also encouraging and terrifying to have David Hidalgo stand on the side of the stage and watch every show we played. He is a genuine musical virtuoso. After a while David always had a guitar in his hand, as he knew we would invite him up to play with us time and again. He actually liked a lot of our stuff and would request to play on certain tunes of ours. Louie would always make time to have conversations with us. He was interested in where we were musically and where we hoped to go with our careers and who our musical influences were. City after city Louie and the Lobos exposed us to their vast and ever-growing network of fans of all racial backgrounds. They—not so incidentally—also exposed us to their favorite restaurants.

Unlike Los Lobos, who were clearly more established, our opening band status did not garner us enough money to cover all of the costs that are incurred on the road. Our revenue barely paid for gas and we most certainly didn't make enough money to pay for hotel rooms, but Los Lobos were always quick to step in. For example, a "rider" is a kind of food and snack hospitality a venue is required to provide for the band and the venue usually knows ahead of time what the band needs as their management or the booking agent provides a detailed list prior to their arrival. Los Lobos of course, always had a great spread. An elaborate array of veggie, meats, sandwich bread, mayonnaise, mustard, tomatoes, beer, wine and yummy juices that the venue was required to provide for them.

On many a night Louie, Steve, or Mando, Los Lobos' tour manager, would come to our dingy dressing room, look at our chips and salsa rider and then invite us to raid their well stocked one. I was most grateful when at the end of the night they would offer their hotel rooms to us. They preferred to drive through the night to their next destination so they would go into their rooms for an hour or two, take showers and then come down to the parking lot and give us their room keys. On these nights we would get to take showers and sleep on clean beds. We would then get up at the crack of dawn and drive to the next town. I will forever be grateful for the generosity they extended to us in those early years.

The last night one of our many runs we played The House of Blues in New Orleans and the Lobos asked what we would like to play with them. Without hesitation we requested, "Be still." As we started to play I felt like that kid on the school bus again as my eyes welled up but this time I was riding the wave of sound right next to them. Here we were playing with the greatest band ever to come out of East L.A! The same legends I had heard in that big yellow bus so many years ago. Mesmerized, I stood next to Louie playing his Candelas *jarana*, David Hidalgo in all his magnificence, the genius of Conrad Lozano, Cesar Rosas, and Steve Berlin it was all too much! We finished our tour and went on to play many more cities without them. Later on, Steve even produced our "Worksongs" album. But these early years remind me of the kind of labor musicians endure night after night. The rigor, the camaraderie, the inspiration for the music itself. I was also fortunate to have been invited to record on "Good Morning, Aztlán" and "The Ride," which has been one of my greatest and most memorable accomplishments.

Los Lobos as Legacy

Many years later—after that fateful bus ride when I was a teenager—the band Quetzal went on to win a Grammy for best Urban Latin and Alternative Rock Album in 2013. At the podium I thanked them for their help and influence. That same year I finished my Ph.D. and now teach Chicano Latino studies courses for Scripps/Claremont College. One of the most popular courses I designed is called, "Chican@ Music: From Genre to Experience." I of course, have a special two weeks devoted exclusively to the trajectory, exploration and enduring body of work that has been generated by Los Lobos. It is never enough time to discuss the depth and power of the lyrics and sonic influences they have generated for more than 40 years. But it helps to reference Louie Pérez's lyrics which brings them closer to an overall understanding of the beauty of our Chicano culture, our depth, and deep commitment to the art of music, community, and familia.

Martha González *is a member of the musical group Quetzal. She teaches at the Claremont Colleges in Claremont, California.*

LET'S PUT AN END TO THIS NIGHTMARE: SCREWY LOUIE'S L.A.

■ *by Elsa Flores Almaráz*

DURING THE MID-1970s, I had the great fortune to receive a job in the arts where I met a lifelong collaborator, Louie Pérez. We met as musicians and artists, and began working together at a local cultural center, *Plaza de La Raza* in East Los Angeles. Along with Louie, David Hidalgo, and Cesar Torres, I taught The History of Mexico Through Music to a constant stream of inner city schoolchildren. We played everything from conch shells to Richie Valens. In doing so Louie and I forged a creative friendship that led us in directions unknown to either of us at the time. Yet we followed our creative impulses. I, camera always in hand, documented Louie's brilliant conceptual performance art pieces from within the confines of cultural institutions to art gallery walls that eventually spilled onto the streets of Los Angeles.

It was one of the most fertile times of our young creative lives in a climate of diversity and expansion in the arts community. Artists banded together to break barriers with experimental works supported and embraced by the arts community. The Chicano punk music movement was brewing, as was a booming gallery scene in Downtown L.A. In 1981 we celebrated the 200th Birthday of Los Angeles. With Los Angeles Bicentennial celebrations staged throughout the City of Angels, artists took up arms in response to the political and cultural history of our city, both the victories as well as the dark underbelly of our city's sordid past.

"Screwy Louie" was born.

With the use of costuming and spontaneous music utilizing everything from prerecorded soundtracks streaming through cassette tape players, toy instruments, and repurposed traditional instrumentation, Louie's genius began to emerge. He transformed into the iconic character, "Screwy Louie," and created a series of performance art pieces entitled "Let's Put An End To This Nightmare," "Screwy Louie for President," "The Knuckleheads" (spontaneous music by Perez, Hidalgo, and Flores), and the Mesoamerican inspired "Aztec Wrestler."

My job was easy, following Louie around and capturing the magic. These performances and stunning visual art pieces fed my soul. The debut performance on September 5, 1980 of "Let's Put an End to This Nightmare" at Los Angeles Contemporary Exhibitions (LACE) Gallery, curated by Carlos Almaráz for an exhibit called "Espina," proved to be a force that could not be contained. A month later Louie took it to the streets of downtown as an expanded performance that led Screwy Louie on a journey through the 2nd Street Tunnel.

Louie created a sculptural prop, a cross that he built utilizing family photos, plaster cast of the artist's own hands and feet, and a hubcap halo crowning the cross. The entire artwork represented a post-modern effigy to "The Crucifixion." With painted calavera face, leather jacket, and Converse kicks, Screwy Louie bared his own cross in a trance-like procession through the 2nd Street Tunnel. This felt like a futurist portal into an otherworldly realm in an act of purification, spiritual purge, and personal exorcism.

Not long after, Louie continued his "Nightmare" campaign and staged a surreal press conference on 8th and Spring streets outside my studio window. It concluded with Louie being overcome by the weight of the nightmare, flyers strewn about as he laid there, another city urchin taking the hit for the collective.

Louie was and continues to be an inspirational force of nature.

Elsa Flores Almaráz *is a Los Angeles based multi-media artist and has creatively collaborated with Louie Perez for nearly 40 years.*

LOUIE PÉREZ: MUSICIAN, ARTIST, AND FRIEND

■ *by Luis J. Rodríguez*

FOR MANY OF US East Los Angeles Chicanos the band Los Lobos was our band, our homies. They were the first *vatos* to make it all the way out of the barrio and back. They reached the pinnacle in the world of popular music. Of course, many had tried before—Little Willie G and Thee Midniters, Cannibal and the Headhunters, Lil' Ray, The Village Callers, El Chicano, Tierra, Los Illegals, Ruben Guevara (of Ruben and the Jets and Con Safos), The Brat, The Plugz, and Califas. Today bands like Quetzal, La Santa Cecilia, Las Cafeteras, and even newer ones such as Chicano Batman, are breaking new ground.

Remarkable musical hybrids burst forth in East L.A., the largest Mexican community in the United States. It has been known as such since Mexicans first settled there in large numbers during the Mexican Revolution and other upheavals from 1910 to 1930, when Mexico lost a million people and there were an estimated one million refugees who came to the United States at a time when Mexico only had 15 million people, about the population of Guatemala today. Los Lobos and the community that spawned them are part of a vital historical continuum.

Chicanos didn't invent Boogie, Rock-n-roll, Hip Hop, Punk, Ska, Cumbia, or Salsa, but we Chicanoized all of it, brought a unique color and flavor, a *cholo/pachuco* sensitivity. We also created lowriders and a street style that has influenced all these musical genres, including what has been called West Coast Hip Hop and Cholo Punk. And Los Lobos and Louie Pérez are the beneficiaries and the benefactors of that cultural dynamic.

I first knew of Los Lobos around the time they started, in the early 1970s, playing for Chicano movement events and family gatherings. My Chicano *compas,* Luis Torres and David Sandoval, produced Los Lobos' first album, "Los Lobos del Este de Los Angeles: Just Another Band From East L.A." It was an independently produced project, which helped Los Lobos come to the attention of a major record label. Torres and Sandoval were mentors of mine in the journalism and broadcasting fields. We were all politically active in the most radical wing of the Chicano movement.

Before I moved to Chicago in May of 1985, the last thing I did was watch Los Lobos at a free concert in Lincoln Park on Los Angeles' eastside, which the Los Angeles Police Department later attacked and shut down following a ruckus at the end of the park. Instead of isolating the problem, police pushed out the mostly peaceful and family-oriented crowd, often with horses and batons as helicopters hovered menacingly overhead.

That's the way it was in East L.A.

About that time I left Los Angeles and lived for 15 years in Chicago. In those years Los Lobos came periodically to that Midwestern city to perform. By then they were known as one of best live bands in the country. They had had an international number one hit, "La Bamba," from the movie about the life of Ritchie Valens. They eventually won Grammys and shared stages with the likes of Bob Dylan, The Grateful Dead, and U2.

When they came to Chicago they would pack the local alternative music clubs in Uptown. Louie Pérez reached out to me in the 1990s after I became known for my poetry and later the best-selling memoir, "Always Running, La Vida Loca, Gang Days in L.A." I got backstage passes and brought my wife, children, and my new Chicago Mexican friends with me. When the band played, the rafters shook to high heaven. People danced, yelled, and I remember seeing Louie Pérez on drums or guitar, the calm eye within this rock-n-roll storm. They also introduced original Spanish language corridos and cumbia numbers that brought the house down.

Louie just played, a depth in his presence. He was always gracious to my entourage and me. Over time we became solid friends.

One time, Louie invited me to meet him in Charlestown, West Virginia where the band was scheduled to play. We were eager to watch the band perform and I took four other Chicanos from Chicago with me. But for some reason Los Lobos never made it. An unforeseen quirk in logistics. Then something kind of crazy happened while I was there. The mostly white patrons of the honky tonk club somehow thought we (my friends and I) were Los Lobos, despite our constant denials. At one point someone on the stage tried to bring us up. Thank God we didn't—Los Lobos would never have been able to play that town again. This incident was the catalyst for one of my signature poems, "A Tale of Los Lobos."

Louie Pérez and I had a productive encounter in Mexico a few years after that.

In 2009, I arrived at the Guadalajara Book Fair, the largest Spanish-language book fair in the Western Hemisphere. I came as part of a team from

Los Angeles that included people from Tia Chucha's Centro Cultural & Bookstore, which my wife Trini and I co-founded in 2001. We also brought the first official lowrider show through the efforts of Chicana Professor Denise Sandoval.

Later we saw Los Lobos in a concert for the book fair that had thousands in attendance. People loved Los Lobos, although years earlier they were apparently not received particularly well by some audiences in Mexico. I recall how badly Mexican media and others would treat their Chicano brethren from "the other side." Chicanos would sometimes be derisively dismissed as "pochos" by Mexican nationals. But by the mid-2000s, there was an opening. Los Lobos had arrived. And even I, a well-known Chicano writer, was treated well, given some 20 media outlets to speak to. Things were changing, mostly due to large numbers of Chicanoized deportees from the United States.

The idea of "The Three Louies" germinated in Guadalajara at dinner with Louie Pérez during the week of the big book fair. After returning to L.A., we reached out to our homie, Luis Torres, who by then was a long-time award-winning journalist. All of us were called "Louie" or some variation of that name. We decided to "perform" on stage in front of audiences, to share our stories. We were three guys named Louie (or Luis) from L.A.'s Eastside who overcame obstacles and had some measure of professional success.

"The Three Louies" was a "conversation" between homeboys where we invited the public to sit in and listen, as if they were eavesdropping on a personal discussion. We made it funny, serious, and poetic, a discourse among East L.A. *carnales* who somehow, and at great odds, carved out places in music, art (Louie Pérez was also an accomplished painter), journalism, and letters. We took "The Three Louies" on the road, as they say, for performances at colleges, bookstores, community centers and even the prestigious Aspen Literary Festival.

Great fun sharing stories and insights with Pérez and Torres.

Now, more than 40 years after Los Lobos began to play as Garfield High School students (and I had removed myself from "La Vida Loca," the crazy gang-drug world I was embroiled in until 1973), Louie Pérez and Los Lobos have left an undeniable and indelible mark in U.S. and world music. That's how the wolf survives.

Luis J. Rodríguez, *the author of more than fifteen books of poetry, fiction and nonfiction, is poet laureate emeritus of the City of Los Angeles.*

MATTER OF TIME: A RECOLLECTION

■ *by Mary Pérez*

IT WAS THREE DAYS before Thanksgiving in 2011. I had just finished a long day of parent/teacher conferences as school counselor at St. Juliana School in Fullerton, California. I stuffed the reports into my briefcase and headed to the school parking lot. I tossed the attaché onto the back seat of the car and put the key into the ignition. The song "A Matter of Time," sung by Elvis Costello, came on the radio and at that moment I found myself transported back in time, which evoked memories that were both joyful and sad.

> *Speak softly, don't wake the baby*
> *Come and hold me once more*
> *Before I have to go.*
> *There is a lot of work out there,*
> *Everything will be fine*
> *And I'll send for you, baby,*
> *In just a matter of time.*

The first time I heard this song I was on my way to Mount Saint Mary's College in Los Angeles, where I was an undergraduate student. It was a cold January morning in 1983. I had just dropped off our six-year-old son at school and entered the Pomona Freeway headed westbound. My husband Louie Pérez had left the night before on a six-week tour of the Midwest. It was midnight and the 15-passenger Dodge van had just arrived to pick him up when he came to our bedroom to say goodbye. He gave me a kiss and whispered, "I left a copy of my new song on the kitchen table." One more kiss and off he went into the night air with his suitcase and a couple of burritos in a brown paper bag.

I put the cassette into the player and listened to the unfinished track. On the cassette David Hidalgo's voice accompanied only by a guitar was singing the lyrics to the song he co-wrote with Louie.

As I traveled through East L.A. and the downtown area of Los Angeles, the lyrics I heard on the car's cassette player began to take on new meaning.

They seemed to narrate everything I passed as I drove to school. I thought of the struggles of an immigrant family being separated by the need to work, a parent leaving home and the ones they love, leaving their country to make a "better life." The exchange between the couple in the song is beautiful and heartbreaking. It paints a portrait of sacrifice on many levels, and it softly echoed our life—Louie's and mine. Truly "A Matter of Time" is an ode to the migrant journey most of our descendants took, either generations ago or more recently. Certainly the song was a metaphoric love letter to my son and me as Louie and I faced a long and arduous period apart during those early years of Los Lobos' touring.

The story of migration transcends many cultural boundaries. Equally, the song has universal appeal. Sung, for example, by Elvis Costello to striking labor unions in England in 1985. It affirms that the historical narrative of the biblical Exodus is not limited to one race or nation. It can be England, Mexico, Syria, El Salvador, or the *barrios* of Los Angeles.

Theologian Walter Brueggeman suggests that as a society we sometimes suffer from a collective amnesia. He describes how people are often forgotten or discarded according to their perceived "usefulness." If we look at the implications of the Exodus, we might see the repetition by and large of mass human flight. Throughout history people have left their homes to escape famine, war, or persecution in search of a "better life."

And parallel to the early migrants of the diaspora, suspicion, exploitation, and hatred have often replaced empathy, community, and contribution.

When I consider the contributions Los Lobos have made, it becomes evident that it is impossible to separate the culture from the music, particularly as seen in the written word. Many of the musical influences originate from the city that Los Lobos grew up in, the variety of music they listened to, the cultural

and spiritual traditions of their childhood that have informed their work.

All of these images become a canvas of beautiful pictures that come alive when you hear their songs. Broadly speaking, these melodies and mantras come from an immigrant story, an immigrant consciousness, and an immigrant community.

The cultural richness of the immigrant community is frequently mitigated by the lived experience of its people. Immigrants are not just the "useful" gardeners, farmworkers, housekeepers, cooks, and janitors. A migrant's contribution is often realized in their poets, playwrights, doctors, lawyers, and in the case of Los Lobos, "just another band from East L.A."

Mary and Louie have been married since 1975.

263